THE RUSSIAN ALBUM

ALSO BY MICHAEL IGNATIEFF

Virtual War: Kosovo and Beyond
Isaiah Berlin: A Life
The Warrior's Honor: Ethnic War and Modern Conscience
Scar Tissue
Blood and Belonging: Journeys into the New Nationalism
The Needs of Strangers
A Just Measure of Pain

Michael Ignatieff

THE RUSSIAN ALBUM

Picador USA
Metropolitan Books
Henry Holt and Company
New York

www.picadorusa.com

Picador® is a U.S. registered trademark and is used by Henry Holt and Company under license from Pan Books Limited.

For information on Picador USA Reading Group Guides, as well as ordering, please contact the Trade Marketing department at St. Martin's Press.
Phone: 1-800-221-7945 extension 763
Fax: 212-677-7456
E-mail: trademarketing@stmartins.com

Parts of the Afterword appeared in somewhat different form in *Blood and Belonging* (BBC Books and Chatto & Windus 1993, Vintage 1994)

ISBN 0-312-28183-8

First published in Great Britain by Chatto & Windus Ltd

First U.S. Edition: June 2001

10 9 8 7 6 5 4 3 2 1

CONTENTS

1   THE BROKEN PATH   1

2   MOTHER AND DAUGHTER   21

3   FATHER AND SON   40

4   PAUL AND NATASHA   66

5   PETROGRAD   86

6   REVOLUTION   108

7   THE CAUCASUS   120

8   SAVAGE LANDS AFAR   144

9   THE LITTLE FOOLS   166

AFTERWORD   187

INDEX   207

ACKNOWLEDGEMENTS

I wish to acknowledge the generosity of the Leverhulme Foundation in supporting research for this book and also the assistance of the Institute for the Study of the USA and Canada, Moscow, during two study tours of the Soviet Union in 1983 and 1986. Neither institution should be held responsible for the facts and opinions contained in this book.

I wish to thank Carmen Callil, Andrew Motion, Elisabeth Sifton, Cynthia Good and Anthony Sheil for advice, criticism and support above and beyond the call of their duties as my editors and agents. My uncles Vladimir, Alec and Lionel Ignatieff and my aunts Florence Hargreaves Ignatieff, Marjorie Adams Ignatieff and Helen Fraser Ignatieff were unstinting in tracking down photographs, manuscripts and missing facts. My wife, Susan Barrowclough, read the manuscript in all its stages and did her best, as usual, to save me from myself. The book is dedicated to my father, who managed to be both detached and helpful, and to my son, who, bless him, couldn't have cared less.

I am grateful to the following copyright holders who have granted permission to reprint material:

'Still Life' from *The House on Marshland* by Louise Gluck, copyright © 1971, 1972, 1973, 1974, 1975 by Louise Gluck. Published by The Ecco Press in 1975.

'The Untelling' from *The Story of Our Lives* by Mark Strand, copyright © 1973 by Mark Strand.

SOURCES

The memoirs of Count Paul and Countess Natasha Ignatieff, upon which this book is based, are on deposit with the Public Archives of Canada in Ottawa.

NOTE

My grandmother was referred to both as Natalie and Natasha. In what follows, I have chosen the Russian form, Natasha.

FOR THEO AND HIS GRANDFATHER

> ... in what shape
> was it we first perceived it – the unstanched
> hereditary thing, working its way
> along the hollows of the marrow ...?

AMY CLAMPITT *'What the Light Was Like'*

IGNATIEFF AND MESTCHERSKY FAMILY TREE

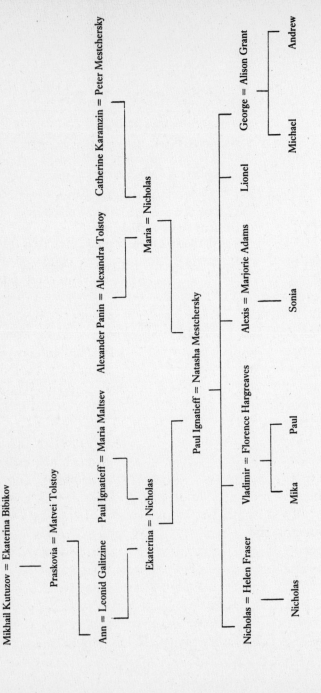

ONE

THE BROKEN PATH

Dwell on the past and you'll lose an eye.
Ignore the past and you'll lose both of them.

OLD RUSSIAN PROVERB

No one I know lives in the house where they grew up or even in the town or village where they once were children. Most of my friends live apart from their parents. Many were born in one country and now live in another. Others live in exile, forming their thoughts in a second language among strangers. I have friends whose family past was consumed in the concentration camps. They are orphans in time. This century has made migration, expatriation and exile the norm, rootedness the exception. To come as I do from a hybrid family of White Russian exiles who married Scottish Canadians is to be at once lucky – we survived – and typical.

Because emigration, exile and expatriation are now the normal condition of existence, it is almost impossible to find the right words for rootedness and belonging. Our need for home is cast in the language of loss; indeed, to have that need at all you have to be already homeless. Belonging now is retrospective rather than actual, remembered rather than experienced, imagined rather than felt. Life now moves so quickly that some of us feel that we were literally different people at previous times in our lives. If the continuity of our own selves is now problematic, our connection with family ancestry is yet more in question. Our grandparents stare out at us from the pages of the family album, solidly grounded in a time now finished, their lips open, ready to speak words we cannot hear.

For many families, photographs are often the only artefacts to survive the passage through exile, migration or the pawnshop. In a secular culture, they are the only household icons, the only objects that perform the religious function of connecting the living to the dead and of locating the identity of the living in time. I never feel I know my friends until either I meet their parents or see their photographs and since this rarely happens, I often wonder whether I know anybody very well. If we are strangers even to our friends, it is because our knowledge of each other is always in a dimension of time that my grandparents' culture would have considered inconceivably shallow. In the world of both the rich and the poor of even a century ago, one knew someone as his father's son, his grandmother's grandson and so on. In the Russian style of address, first name and then patronymic, this kind of knowing is inscribed in the very way one names a friend or relation. To a Russian, I am Michael Georgevitch, George's son, a self rooted in a family past. In the non-Russian world I live in, I am known for what I do, for how I am now, not for the past I embody. Looking at someone's family album is a way towards a deeper temporal knowing of another. But nowadays, a frontier of intimacy has to be crossed before these photographs are shown even to friends. Within the family itself, photographs are not really icons, hovering presences on the wall. Styles of inheritance are now individual: we are free to take or refuse our past. Children have as much right to refuse interest in these icons as they have to stick to their own opinions. Yet the more negotiable, the more invented the past becomes, the more intense its hold, the more central its invention becomes in the art of making a self. Eventually there are few of us who do not return home one holiday weekend, go to the bottom drawer, pull out the old shoe box and spread the pictures around us on the floor.

Father has his arm around Tereze
She squints. My thumb
is in my mouth: my fifth autumn.
Near the copper beech
the spaniel dozes in the shadows.
Not one of us does not avert his eyes.
                    (Louise Gluck, 'Still Life')

From its beginnings, photography was recognized as a new source of consciousness about the family past. As a contributor to *Macmillan's Magazine* wrote in 1877: 'Anyone who knows what the worth of family affection is among the lower classes and who has seen the array of little portraits over a labourer's fire place will perhaps feel with me that in counteracting the tendencies, social and industrial, which are every day sapping the healthier family affections, the sixpenny photograph is doing more for the poor than all the philanthropists in the world' (quoted in Susan Sontag, *On Photography*). In democratizing the privilege of a family portrait gallery, the sixpenny photograph deserves a place in the social history of modern individualism. With the coming of the photograph, poor families had a new kind of inheritance: sixpenny tokens coded with the signs of their genetic legacy. If they could not bequeath property, they could bequeath the history of the handing down of the curve of a lip, the shape of a forehead, the set of a jaw. In giving silent presence to vanished generations and in diffusing this presence throughout the whole culture, photography has played a part in bringing the problem of personal identity to the centre of cultural concern. The aware-ness that we must create ourselves and find our own belonging was once the privilege of an educated elite and is now a general-ized cultural condition. For in helping to constitute identity in time, photography also poses the problem of the freedom of the self to make its own present. To look at an old photograph and to discover that one has inherited the shape of one's eyes, to hear from one's parents that one has also inherited a temperament, is both to feel a new location in time but also a dawning sense of imprisonment. The passion for roots – the mass pastime of family history – represses the sense of suffocation that family photographs can engender. That is one reason why the old photographs get consigned to the old shoe box at the bottom of the drawer. We need them but we do not want to be claimed by them. Because they bring us face to face with an inheritance that cannot be altered, photographs pose the problem of freedom: they seem to set the limits within which the self can be created.

The photographs in a family album bring us closer to the past and yet their acute physical tactility reminds us of all the distance that still remains uncrossed. As such, photographs have done something to create that very modern sense of the past as a lost country. My first impression of that sense came when I was very young. I was watching an interview on television with an old black man who was supposed to be the last American who had lived under slavery. In a whisper, he told how he had been born in what must now be Liberia and how he had been enticed onto a ship with promises of corn fritters growing on trees in a land where you never had to work all day. I can remember thinking that if this tiny man with his faint voice and papery skin were to die, the past of slavery, the chains and the chanting, would slide away from me like a cliff subsiding into the sea. I still cannot shake off the superstition that the only past that is real, that exists at all, is the one contained within the memories of living people. When they die, the past they hold within them simply vanishes, and those of us who come after cannot inherit their experience, only preserve the myth of its existence. We can mark the spot where the cliff was washed away by the sea, but we cannot repair the wound the sea has made. In my lifetime the last of the people born before the Russian Revolution will die. My father is the very last of that generation, aged four in February 1917, just old enough to remember the bayonets glinting like glass below the window of the house in Petrograd on the morning the soldiers stormed to the Duma and said they had had enough of hunger and war. His memory just bestrides this abyss dividing everything before and everything after the revolution. I in turn am the last generation to know his generation, the last to be able to plumb their memory, to feel the presence of their past in the timbre of their voices and in the gaze they cast back across time. Already I am so far away from what happened, so much a Canadian born of this time and place and no other, that I feel fraudulent in my absorption in the vanishing experience of another generation. Yet so swiftly does time move now that unless I do my work to preserve memory, soon all there will be left is photographs and photographs only document the distance that time has travelled; they cannot bind past and present together with meaning.

I am a historian and historians are supposed to believe that they can transport themselves in time to recapture experience swept away by the death of earlier generations. In even the most rigorously scientific history, there is a resurrectionary hope at work, a faith in the power of imagination and empathy to vault the gulf of time. To do their work at all, historians have to believe that knowledge can consummate desire – that our dull and patient immersion in the records of the past can ultimately satisfy our desire to master time's losses. The historical imagination emerges from loss, dispossession and confinement, the same experiences which make for exile and migration. It is roused when the past can no longer be taken for granted as a felt tradition or when the past has become a burden from which the present seeks emancipation. It is a sense of fracture or a sense of imprisonment that sends historians back to the archives, the memoirs, the tape-recorded voices. Yet this relation between loss and the imagination is full of irony. History has less authority than memory, less legitimacy than tradition. History can never speak with the one voice that our need for belonging requires. It cannot heal the hurt of loss. Our knowledge of the past cannot satisfy our desire for the past. What we can know about the past and what we want from it are two different things.

Photographs of ancestors seem to capture this irony precisely.

In the family album, my grandfather seems almost real, almost on the point of speaking. But his clothes, the frock coat, the hands held down the striping of his court uniform, mark him as a historical being irrevocably distant in time. The more palpable the photograph renders his presence, the more sharply I realize that the gulf that divides us involves both my mortality and theirs.

That it is *my* death which is in question, and not just his, becomes apparent when we look at photographs of ourselves. They awaken a sense of loss because they work against the integrative functions of forgetting. Photographs are the freeze frames that remind us how discontinuous our lives actually are. It is in a tight weave of forgetting and selective remembering that a continuous self is knitted together. Forgetting helps us to sustain a suspension of belief in our own death which allows us time to believe in our lives. At the end of his life, the French writer Roland Barthes gave a talk to an audience much younger than himself, and thought out loud about the hope – and the passion for life – that forgetting makes possible: 'In order to live, I have to forget that my body has a history. I have to throw myself into the illusion that I am the contemporary of these young bodies who are present and listening to me, and not of my own body weighed down with the past. From time to time, in other words, I have to be born again, I have to make myself younger than I am. I let myself be swept along by the force of all living life – forgetting' (*Nouvel Observateur*, 31 March 1980).

Photographs do not always support the process of forgetting and remembering by which we weave an integral and stable self over time. The family album does not always conjure forth the stream of healing recollection that binds together the present self and its past. More often than not photographs subvert the continuity that memory weaves out of experience. Photography stops time and serves it back to us in disjunctive fragments. Memory integrates the visual within a weave of myth. The knitting together of past and present that memory and forgetting achieve is mythological because the self is constantly imagined, constructed, invented out of what the self wishes to remember. The photograph acts towards the self like a harshly lit mirror, like the historian confronted with the wish-fulfilments of nationalistic fable or political lie. Look at a picture of yourself at four or five, and ask yourself honestly whether you can feel that you still are this tender self, squinting into the camera. As a record of our forgetting, the camera has played some part in engendering our characteristic modern suspicion about the self-deceiving ruses of our consciousness. Memory heals the scars of time. Photography documents the wounds.

So it is not only the dead ancestors who seem as distant as stars but even the younger versions of ourselves who take up our positions in the family album. It is this double process of loss, the loss of them, the loss of oneself, which the struggle of writing tries to arrest.

> His pursuit was a form of evasion.
> The more he tried to uncover
> the more there was to conceal
> the less he understood.
> If he kept it up
> he would lose everything.
> He knew this
> and remembered what he could –
> always at a distance,
> on the other side of the lake,
> or across the lawn,
> always vanishing, always there.
>   (Mark Strand, 'The Untelling')

Yet loss is only one of the emotions awakened by exile and dispossession. There is also the 'syncopal kick', the release of stored energies that Vladimir Nabokov describes in *Speak Memory* as being one of exile's least expected gifts. It was exile that made Nabokov a writer; it was exile that turned the taken-for-granted past into a fabled territory that had to be reclaimed, inch by inch, by the writer's art. Just as in the moment of flight exiles must grab the treasures that will become their belongings on the road into exile, so they must choose the past they will carry with them, what version they will tell, what version they will believe. From being an unconsidered inheritance, the past becomes their invention, their story.

Once the story has been handed on from first to second generation, the family past becomes still less a fate and ever more a narrative of self-invention. For someone like myself in the second generation of an émigré tradition, the past has become the story we write to give weight and direction to the accident and contingency of our lives. True, we cannot invent our past out of nothing: there are photos and memories and stories, and sometimes our invention consists mostly in denying what it is we have inherited. Yet even when we disavow it, we are inventing a past in our denials. The problem of invention is authenticity. In the second generation we are free to choose our pasts, but the past we choose can never quite seem as real, as authentic, as those of the first generation.

In my own case, I have two pasts. My mother's family, the Grants and the Parkins, were high-minded Nova Scotians who came to Toronto in the last century and made a name for themselves as teachers and writers. They were close to me as a child: as close as my grandmother's house on Prince Arthur Avenue in Toronto.

My father's past is Russian. My grandfather Paul Ignatieff was Minister of Education in the last Cabinet of Tsar Nicholas II. His father, Nicholas Ignatieff, was the Russian diplomat who in 1860 negotiated the Amur-Ussuri boundary treaty that defines the border between Russia and China in the Pacific region to this day; in 1878 he negotiated the treaty bringing the Russo-Turkish War to a conclusion; and in 1881 he was the minister who put his name to the special legislation against the Jews.

My grandmother was born Princess Natasha Mestchersky on an estate near Smolensk bequeathed to her mother's family by

Empress Catherine the Great in the late eighteenth century. In her family she counted a chancellor of Russia, a general who put down the peasant rebellion of Pugachev and the first modern historian of her country, Nicholas Karamzin.

When my Russian grandfather was nineteen and choosing a career, the tramlines of his past ran straight into the future: he would enter a Guards regiment like his father, grandfather and great-grandfather before him. He could then make a career in the army or return to the family estates and live as a gentleman farmer. At some point in his life he would be expected to leave the estate and serve the Tsar, as his grandfather and father had done. He would 'shoulder the chains of service'. It is in these precise senses – a destiny inherited and shouldered without questioning – that his identity is irrevocably different from my own. My identity – my belonging to the past he bequeathed me – is a matter of choosing the words I put on a page. I am glad that this is so: his is not a fate or an identity which I would wish as my own. But it is a difference that makes full understanding between us impossible.

My grandmother's self was made within a frame of choices even narrower than those of her husband: to be a dutiful daughter and then a faithful wife. The fulcrum of her life, the one moment when fate could be heaved this way or that, was marriage. There would be some choosing for her to do, among the young officers with wasp-waisted uniforms who were allowed to dance with her at the Petersburg debutante balls. But she was a Princess Mestchersky and once her eyes had fallen on a man, his particulars 'back to Adam and Eve' would be investigated and if they were found wanting, she would have to choose again.

Both of them were born into a time when their past was also their future. Life had a necessity to it: it was not a tissue of their own making. They grew up in a time measured by a protocol of family decorum. They ended their lives in the formless time of exile, a time with no future and a past suspended out of reach. When they landed in England in the summer of 1919 they were already too old to start again, too old to feel the emancipating energies of exile. My grandparents could only remember: they could no longer invent the present.

Between my two pasts, the Canadian and the Russian, I felt I had to choose. The exotic always exerts a stronger lure than the familiar and I was always my father's son. I chose the vanished past, the past lost behind the revolution. I could count on my mother's inheritance: it was always there. It was my father's past that mattered to me, because it was one I had to recover, to make my own.

My earliest memories are not memories of myself, but of my father talking about his ancestors. I recall being on board the *Queen Mary* during a crossing between New York and Southampton in 1953 when I was six and hearing my father tell the story of how his grandfather Nicholas rode from Peking to Petersburg in six weeks to bring the Tsar the news of the treaty he had signed with the Chinese Emperor; and how when a blizzard struck on the Siberian plains Nicholas had formed his Cossack horsemen into a circle, bivouacked in the centre and warmed themselves through the blizzard by the breath from the horses.

Since my father was a diplomat who moved every eighteen months of my childhood, the things I came to count on as icons of stability were not the houses we lived in, since they changed all the time, but the very few Russian objects we carried with us from one posting to the next. There was a silver ewer and basin that stood on a succession of dining tables in a succession of official apartments, which had once been used by my maternal great-grandmother to wash her hands when she awoke at her country estate in the mornings during the 1880s. Objects like the silver ewer and basin, like the Sultan's diamond star that my mother wore on family occasions, were vital emblems of continuity in a childhood without fixed landmarks. Few of these were still left: some embossed volumes of Nicholas Karamzin's history of Russia, an icon or two on the wall above my parents' bed. Sometimes these objects turned up in family photographs. I still remember the pleasure I got as a child from discovering that a piece of jewellery my mother wore was to be seen in a photograph of my grand-mother Natasha taken seventy years before. It was as if the little pearl and diamond brooch had flown free of its amber imprison-ment in the photograph, vaulting all the time between me and her.

I heard very little Russian as a child: my father did not speak it at home. I went with him to the Russian church in the cities where I grew up – New York, Toronto, Ottawa, Belgrade, Paris, Geneva and London – and I was moved by the service because I did not understand it. Standing beside him in the church, watching him light his candles, say his prayers and sing in his deep vibrating voice, I always felt that he had slipped away through some invisible door in the air. Yet he kept his distance from the Russian émigré community, from their factional intrigues and antedilu-vian politics. He presented himself to the world throughout my childhood as the model of an assimilated Canadian professional. And to this day he is a much more patriotic and sentimental Canadian than I am. For him Canada was the country that gave him a new start. For me, being a Canadian was just one of those privileges I took for granted.

Father often met Soviet diplomats in his work and they always spoke Russian together. Yet the meetings were edgy. I remember one Soviet diplomat, dressed like a Zürich banker with a large black onyx ring on his finger, being introduced to both of us in a lobby of the United Nations building in New York. He doffed his astrakhan and in a great sweeping gesture said in English, 'As the son of a peasant I salute you.' Other Soviets treated the family past with the same mixture of respect and irony. In 1955, my father returned to the Soviet Union as part of an official Canadian delegation led by the Foreign Minister, Mike Pearson. The Soviet officials, led by Nikita Khrushchev himself, called my father *Graf* (Count) and took him aside and asked in all sincerity why he didn't come 'home' again and continue the diplomatic work of his grandfather instead of serving the diplomacy of a small satellite state of the Americans. But my father didn't feel at home at all in the Soviet Union of the 1950s. Even the moments of memoried connection were brief, as when he was shown into his room at the Hotel Astoria in Leningrad, frozen in its pre-revolutionary decor, and saw on the writing desk two silver bears exactly like two little bears that had once stood on his father's desk in the same city forty years before. On that visit, he also realized how archaic his Russian sounded to Soviet citizens and how rusty it had become. He found himself stumbling in his native tongue.

Back home, family feeling on the Russian side was intense, but there were few actual occasions when we came together. Throughout my childhood, the Russian half of the family was scattered abroad. My father's eldest brother, Nicholas, had died in my childhood, and the remaining four were thousands of miles apart. When the brothers did come together for the wedding of my cousin Mika, we all made a little space for them apart and they sat on the couch, balding giants each over six feet tall, talking in Russian, while none of us understood a word. They had all married outside the Russian circle and so none of their children grew up in the Russian tongue. I never learned the language.

In my inability to learn Russian, I can now see the extent of my resistance to a past I was at the same time choosing as my own. The myths were never forced upon me so my resistance was directed not at my father or my uncles but rather at my own inner craving for these stories, at what seemed a weak desire on my part to build my little life upon the authority of their own. I wasn't sure I had the right to the authority of the past and even if I did have the right, I didn't want to avail myself of the privilege. Yet as one of my friends wryly says when I talk like this, no one ever gives up his privileges. So I used the past whenever I needed to, but with a guilty conscience. My friends had suburban pasts or pasts they would rather not talk about. I had a past of Tsarist adventurers, survivors of revolutions, heroic exiles. Yet the stronger my need for them, the stronger too became my need to disavow them, to strike out on my own. To choose my past meant to define the limits of its impingement upon me.

My father always said that I was more Mestchersky than Ignatieff, more like his mother than his father. Since he was more Ignatieff than Mestchersky, the statement underlined how complicated the ties of filiation really were between us. Inheritance is always as much a matter of anxiety as pride. If I was a Mestchersky what could I possibly make of myself? How could I ever master my temperament, that tightly strung bundle of fears and anxieties that seemed to have me locked in its grasp? From the beginning, the project of finding out about my past was connected to a struggle to master the anxiety of its influence.

I also found myself face to face with what I liked least about myself. My grandfather's favourite phrase was, 'Life is not a game, life is not a joke. It is only by putting on the chains of service that man is able to accomplish his destiny on earth.' When Paul talked like this, my grandmother Natasha always used to mutter, 'The Ignatieffs would make hell out of Paradise.'

Early on I learned that both my father and my uncle Nicholas had wanted to write a history of the family. My father had even been to Bulgaria to research the story of his grandfather's role in the creation of Bulgaria after the Russian defeat of the Turks in the war of 1877–78. Nicholas had had similar ideas, but he was dead and his manuscripts lay in his widow's basement. My father was a busy man and his project languished. So the idea of a history of the family had germinated: it was an idea I could bring to fruition if I wanted to. But I held back.

I was in my teens when I first read my grandparents' memoirs. Beginning in September 1940 in a cottage in Upper Melbourne, Quebec, my grandmother Natasha typed out a stream of free associations, beginning with childhood on the estate, her marriage to my grandfather Paul Ignatieff, life in Petersburg, revolution, civil war and escape. She wrote in the English she had learned from her governess, in the English she knew her

grandchildren would grow up speaking. When she got to 1919 –
when she got to the moment they left Russia – she stopped.
Everything became harder then, harder to say and all the period
in exile she left in silence. By then there were over 250 pages, a
jumble that my aunt Florence sorted and retyped after her death.

My grandfather Paul had written his memoirs in Sussex and in
Paris during the 1920s. He wrote in Russian and only much later
translated them into English with the help of a Canadian friend.
My grandmother's recollections are a frank and faithful echo of
the woman she was, put down just as she spoke in every
meandering turn of phrase, but his dry, orderly and restrained
prose was, or so I felt, an exercise in discretion and concealment.
He confined himself to his official career, as gentleman farmer,
governor of Kiev province, deputy Minister of Agriculture and
Minister of Education in the final Cabinet of the Tsar. It is a
restrained public document. Emotion cracks through the shell of
measured phrases just once, when he describes his last meeting
with Nicholas II in the final days of the regime.

Their memoirs were unpublishable, hers because what made
them so alive also made them unreadable, his because they so
meticulously excluded the personal and because the events he
described had been so exhaustively retold in the deluge of Tsarist
memoir. I decided, nearly ten years ago now, to retell their story
in my own words. As a historian, I thought my first task would be
to locate them in their historical setting, to distance myself from
them as members of my family and to treat them instead as
historical specimens, as objects of study. It took me some time
to realize the unintended consequences of this strategy. I can
remember a moment during the early days of my research when I
was reading the proceedings of a Russian land-reform commission of 1902, searching for a mention of the family estates
through spools of faint microfilm. Since my grandfather was a
local marshal of nobility, he had to write a report for the
commission. It was the first time I had read something by him that
was not addressed to his family: the memoirs, the letters I had

read before all had us as their intended audience. In this little report he was suddenly a tiny figure in a historical setting. The irony was that the process of tracking him into his historical context did not make the contours of his character come into sharper relief. The reverse occurred. The more I came to know about him as a historical being – as a quite typical member of the liberal service gentry, as a non-party constitutional monarchist – the more he began to slip out of reach. The sharper I drew his definition as a historical being, the more blurred he became as my grandfather. As an object of historical knowledge he could only be grasped in the plural; as an object of desire, I sought him in his singularity. In the process of finding him as an exemplary imperial character, I lost him as my grandfather. The historical way of knowing the past is to place a figure in the background of serial time; I wanted the opposite, to make him present in simultaneous time with me. Yet I always knew that this was an impossible desire and that even a history of their lives was doomed to failure. I could never recreate the past as my uncles remembered it or hope to conciliate the quarrels between contending memories. Even today the brothers still argue heatedly about some things and I could not hope to establish who was right. Most of all, I could not hope to bring back Paul and Natasha. Even the simplest physical detail about them, how she moved the hair off her face, how he used to snap a book shut when he had read it, required acts of painstaking reconstitution for me; for my father these details were such simple primary memories he scarcely bothered to mention them. It soon became apparent that the only portrait I could hope to paint of Paul and Natasha would always be a crude sketch, a study in the unbridgeable distances between first and second generations. For a long time I thought that if a history was doomed to failure anyway, I should abandon history and turn my grandparents' life into fiction. It was a tempting idea: my characters would be just sufficiently grounded in a real past to be authentic and yet they would do my bidding. They would wear my clothes, speak my lines, live out my dramas and fulfil my ambitions. In creating them I would create myself. In the end the idea of fiction foundered on the realization that such a novel would be peopled by characters neither real in themselves nor faithful to their originals.

It was years before I began to see Paul and Natasha apart from my needs for them. I learned that their lives were not an adventure that existed so that I could quarry them for meanings of my own. There were too many silences, too many things I could not know about them for me to ransack their experience for my purposes. Very slowly, it dawned on me that instead of *them* owing me the secret of my life, I owed *them* fidelity to the truth of the lives they had led. Fiction would have been a betrayal. I had to return and stay close to the initial shock of my encounter with their photographs: that sense that they were both present to me in all their dense physical actuality and as distant as stars. In recreating them as truthfully as I could, I had to respect the distance between us. I had to pay close attention to what they left unsaid; I had to put down a marker at the spots that had not been reclaimed by memory. I could not elide these silences by the artifice of fiction.

I went twice with my father to the Soviet Union to find their traces. There was a lot to find: until the fall of Khrushchev the folk drama of socialist reconstruction justified the levelling of palaces and the conversion of churches to printing plants or lumberyards. Only poverty and backwardness saved old buildings. A country too poor to replace them lived out the drama of the new in the tattered stage sets of the old. In the late 1960s and 1970s, the vandalism of Khrushchevian modernism produced a counter-reaction that reached back to national traditions untarnished by Communism. Now not just the great palaces and monasteries were regilded but anything with a patina of age began to reacquire authority. A new national past uniting pre- and post-1917 was constructed by artful elision of the revolution's destructive work. As a result of this ironic and uneasy attempt to recuperate the Tsarist past, in some ways it is easier to find traces of a Tsarist family past in the Soviet Union than it is in the West. In the leafy shade of the cemetery of Novodevichy convent in Moscow, near the graves of Khrushchev and Stalin's wife, we found the grave of the family renegade, Uncle Alyosha, who began his career as a Tsarist officer and ended it as a Red general. In Leningrad, we found the family house on Fourstatskaya street where my father had watched the first demonstrations of the February Revolution in 1917. It is now the Leningrad Palace of Marriages. In the ballroom where my grandmother once served tea, young couples were being married, one pair every ten minutes, by an imposing woman in a red ball gown and a sash of office. Downstairs in the schoolroom where my uncles used to take their lessons from their French tutor, Monsieur Darier, mothers with pins in their mouths were making last-minute adjustments to their daughters' wedding dresses. And down a small back hallway, with dim portraits of Lenin on the wall and an Intourist calendar of scenes from a Crimean resort, my father found the room that had been his nursery.

In Kislovodsk, a south Caucasus spa town between the Black and Caspian Seas, one September afternoon, my father and I found the green gate of the garden in which stood the house he had lived in with his family during the civil war in 1917 and 1918. Several houses had been crammed into the garden since the family's wretched years there, but there were still apple trees and poplars at the back, just as there were in 1918.

Yet the apparent ease with which we picked up the traces of the family past inside the Soviet Union proved deceptive. I remember suddenly feeling the unseen distances separating me from my past while standing in front of the Matisse paintings in the Pushkin Museum in Moscow, all collected by Tsarist merchants before the First World War. For Russian visitors to the museum, the Matisses are a strange and discordant departure from the realism of Russian nineteenth-century genre painting; they are equally alien to the socialist realism that was to carry this tradition forward in the Soviet period. For Russians, the Matisses are thus fragments of modernism suspended out of reach of the European tradition that nurtured them. For us the Matisse paintings are the founding canvases of our very way of seeing. As I looked at the sunlit ateliers, the bright deck chair, the bowl of flowers, the woman in the lustrous blue dress and looked at the dates of their composition, 1910, 1911, 1912, I realized that they were collected by my grandparents' generation. This generation was the first to have successfully resolved the old dilemma of whether Russians were a European or an Asian people. Natasha spoke and thought in German and English; her dentist was an American who lived in Dresden; she bought her lingerie in Nice; she had Lyle's Golden Syrup for tea in her nursery. Paul was raised by French tutors and grew up thinking and speaking in French. Yet both were passionately attached to the religions, customs, smells, architecture, curses and chaos of their native land.

They travelled across an open frontier to countries whose painting, food and landscape they regarded as their own. Matisse's Mediterranean light was as much their own as the eternal summer light of Petersburg. They were the first generation to reconcile their European and their Russian identities, and they were the last. A border of barbed wire, searchlights and gun emplacements has been sawed across a Europe they once believed stretched from Moscow to the Atlantic, and when I try to follow their footsteps across that frontier I am aware that I am entering a country that now seems more a strange new Asian empire than an old heartland of European culture. The distance that I now must try to cross between them and me is much more than the distance of time. It is the chasm marked by the no man's land of barbed wire that divides European culture into two armed camps.

My Soviet guides were often unsettled by my estrangement from their native land. They wanted to help my search for connections, phoning local history museums to find the new names of streets we knew only from their original names in the 1914 edition of Baedeker's guide to Russia, and helping us even to find the jails and interrogation rooms where my grandfather spent the loneliest hours of his life in 1918. The Soviet guides admired my father's slightly old-fashioned Russian, so much softer and gentler in enunciation than their own, and they were puzzled but polite when I said I understood not a word of my father's native tongue. There were a few sites that it was not possible to visit – Kroupodernitsa, the Ignatieff estate in the Ukraine where my great-grandfather and great-grandmother are buried, seemed to be off limits, though for reasons that were never explained. Yet the authorities sent a photographer to the village church and took pictures of the family graves, dressed with bouquets of fresh flowers. We were told the estate is now a village school. Of Doughino, the eighteenth-century estate near Smolensk where my grandmother grew up, there was no trace. It was burned to the ground in 1917. My father wept when he left Russia, and I left dry-eyed.

There must be something to the superstition that by returning to a place one can return in time to the self one once was in those places. My father was six when he left Russia in 1919, and his memories are few and indistinct. Yet he found a catharsis in returning, a rounding out of his life. For me, the trips to the Soviet Union redoubled my sense of the irrecoverable distance of my family past. But by a paradox that must be at the heart of writing itself, the more distant everything became, the more urgent it became to get the story down before the death of my father's generation broke the last living links.

My father and his brothers gave me every kind of help but they could not conceal their misgivings. I was like an auctioneer sent to value their treasures for sale. Our long sessions together over the tape recorder were harbingers of their mortality. I often thought that it would be better if I left the project aside until they were safely dead and buried. Then I would be free to say it all. But what kind of freedom is that, the freedom to say everything one never dared to say in person? Who is not haunted by the silences, the missed chances for truth that slip between father and son, mother and daughter, the chances that slip finally into the grave? I do not want to miss my chance.

I have done my best to disentangle history from myth, fact from fancy, but in the end I cannot be sure of the truth, either of what happened or what is remembered. I wasn't there. I can only register the impact of their struggle to remember: I can tell them the wave did reach the shore. Because Paul and Natasha managed to remember what they did and passed it on, I owe to them the conviction that my own life did not begin with my birth, but with hers and with his, a hundred years ago in a foreign land, and that now as the last of the generation who knew what life was like behind the red curtain of the revolution begins to depart, it is up to me to pass on their remembering to whoever comes after.

After all these years spent searching for their traces, I can hear their voices at last as if they were in the room. This is how Natasha began her memoirs, her first sentence:

'I decide while I am still in my fresh mind to put down all dates and years of main episodes of our lives, my dear husband's and mine, so that when we pass into eternity our sons and their families may have a picture more or less of interesting episodes of our lives, colourful lives, thanks to so many striking events and in the middle age of our lives tremendous upheavals we had to pass through and which left a totally different side of our further existence.'

TWO
MOTHER AND DAUGHTER
———

Summer mornings at the Mestchersky country estate in the 1880s began with the same ritual. Natasha and her sister Vera, already washed, combed and dressed by their nurse, would file into their mother's bedroom and kiss her good morning. Their mother would then sit up in bed and swallow a raw egg. The maid brought it in a glass on a silver tray and her mother would down it with a brisk, convulsive snort. The maid would then pour warm water from a ewer into a silver basin and Natasha's mother would wash her hands. Natasha and her sister Vera sat on the end of the bed and watched.

The silver ewer and basin are just about the only things that have survived from those mornings at Doughino, the family estate in the western Russian province of Smolensk. They are plain, unadorned rectangular shapes, embossed with the family coat of arms. They used to stand on the dining-room table in our house in Ottawa and my mother used the jug for flowers. I have a memory from my early childhood of curling red petals, musty and fragrant, collecting in the silver of that basin.

After the egg and the washing of the hands, the maid brought Natasha, Vera and their mother cups of Ceylon tea, with scalded cream from the estate dairy. While their mother's jet-black hair was being braided, piled in two tight buns above her ears, she fired questions at Natasha and Vera: had they said their prayers? Were they washed? Were they ready for their lessons? The two little girls in their pinafores held hands and replied in unison. It was a family joke that when spoken to they always chimed in together with voices like mice. Their mother beckoned them closer, straightened their pinafores, took Natasha's hair between her fingers: why did it never curl? Natasha must have another session with Miss Saunders's curling iron.

When the butler appeared with the morning's post on a tray, the two girls were dismissed with a peck on the forehead. From her bed their mother dictated her correspondence to a secretary and the girls went off to the schoolroom for their lessons with Miss Saunders and later with Mr Sharples, the English tutor. They kept up English ways in the nursery – bread pudding with Lyle's Golden Syrup, Huntley & Palmer biscuits in square red tins from the English shops in Moscow.

Natasha was born Princess Mestchersky in August 1877, into a family of six girls and two boys: Katherine, Alexander (known as Sasha), Sonia, Maria, Sophia, Peter, Vera and Natasha. She was the last, the little gawky one, a child of middle age. Her mother, Maria Panin, was a descendant of Nikita Panin, Catherine the Great's chancellor whose brother, General Peter Panin, had led the troops in the suppression of the uprising of the peasant bandit Pugachev in the 1780s. Doughino, the family estate, was a gift to the Panins from the Empress. Natasha's father, Prince Nicholas Mestchersky, was rector of Moscow University.

Only one photograph remains of Natasha's mother and father. They are seated side by side on a couch at Doughino. He is thin, fine-boned and long in the face. His long white beard trails down the front of his frock coat. He is bending to graze his wife's hand with his lips. His eyes gaze at her devotedly. She does not spare him a glance. She stares out at the camera, massive, stout and ugly with highly polished black ankle boots poking out beneath her black taffeta dress. Her black hair is pulled back in a tight bun; her cheeks are heavy; her lidded eyes appraise the photographer with lofty amusement. The Panins had once been Panini and had come to Russia from Italy some time in the seventeenth century to make their fortune. From them, Natasha's mother had inherited dark olive skin and a passion for argument. Her daughters said she had a 'man's brain'; she was impatient of the coy and innocent vagueness of the women of her time and class. Ugly and vivacious, imperious and argumentative, she ruled Doughino in the summers and the upper reaches of Moscow society in the winters. Together with Countess Sheremetieff and a Miss Tuitcheff, she made up a trio known as the '*conseil des infaillibles*' in the Moscow society of the 1880s. They were the court of final instance on manners, deportment and marriages. She was famous in her heyday for the sharpness of her tongue. Once when old Prince Volkonsky took her hand at a dinner party and began to tell her unsavoury Moscow gossip, she reached into her reticule, pulled out a small padlock and handed it to him, saying tartly in French that if he couldn't stop telling tales about his friends, he should keep his mouth shut. She dominated them all, husband, children, servants: every summer the married daughters were commanded to appear at Doughino with their husbands and children from the four corners of western Russia, with nurses and governesses, tutors and coachmen, to spend the summer together under her watchful and disapproving eye.

Natasha's father was a mild old gentleman of conventional opinions, ruled by his wife and his daughters. Natasha took after him in looks and temperament: high forehead, long straight nose, tall and thin-boned. His only apparent role in his children's upbringing was to line them up in his study every morning and administer a spoonful of cod-liver oil followed by a slice of black bread to take away the taste.

He was generous and absent-minded, always doling out money to the Moscow beggars when out on his morning walk to the university. Once when Natasha was with him, a beggar approached and when her father replied ruefully that he had forgotten to carry any change, the beggar replied that he had plenty; Natasha's father stood there smiling absently while the beggar took the ruble note and handed back enough kopecks to make the transaction satisfactory to both sides. In matters of charity, as in matters of the home, Natasha's father was a patriarch ruled by others.

Natasha's father had a brother as scabrous as he was respectable. An anti-Semitic homosexual, always in the company of young Guards officers, he was known in Petersburg circles as the Prince of Sodom. He was also the editor of *The Citizen* (*Grazhdanin*), required reading for the reactionaries of his epoch. Because of Uncle Vladimir, 'a certain kind of citizen' became the Mestchersky code-phrase for homosexuals. 'Petty informer, tattler, toady, a creature of perverted sexual taste, pulp novelist, embezzler' – the gossips did not spare him. It was said his wife had caught him *in flagrante* with a trumpet player of the Guards. It was whispered the Prince also dressed up in women's clothes. Yet his morals apparently did not bother those who read him for his opinions. After the assassination of the Liberator Tsar in 1881, Vladimir Mestchersky wrote an editorial in *The Citizen* which brayed out the master theme of a new epoch: 'Everywhere one goes, only a single cry is heard from the people: Beat them! Beat them! In answer to this what do the authorities reply? Anything except the birch. What is the result of this contradiction? A terrible lack of discipline, the destruction of the father's authority within the family, drunkenness, crime and so on . . .'

When the new Tsar, Alexander III, took the throne in 1881, there were few makers of opinion more to his taste than Prince Mestchersky. Natasha's father and mother refused to receive the old debaucher in their home, yet they seem to have shared most of his views, though in milder form.

The Mestcherskys were a family of highly strung hypochondriacs. Like most Russian families of the time, they called doctors at the slightest cough or fever. In their case, however, family anxieties about health had some foundation. Natasha's oldest sister, Katherine, had gone to a hotel in Ostend to take the sea air and had died of 'galloping consumption' (tuberculosis) at the age of twenty; in their grief, Natasha's mother and father watched over their remaining children with obsessive attention. The next daughter, Maria, had been invalided by a riding accident and was taken on a round-the-world tour by her mother to recover. The older son, Sasha, a stooping giant six foot six inches tall, was a mild and gentle character whose passion was his mother's green-houses: he grew carnations from cuttings and became a fanatic for the colour green, wearing a suite of green baize with a green deerstalker hat and experimenting with all the variations of green orchids. His favourite dish was pea soup.

An English tutor was hired to turn this shy and peculiar boy into a gentleman fit for a career. No one ever knew quite what happened – Natasha's mother could not bear to discuss it – but the tutor took to beating Sasha for every mistake in lessons and for every bout of masturbation in bed. The boy would have silently endured this routine had he not succumbed to menin-gitis. When he recovered the truth came out, the tutor was dismissed, and the parents reconciled themselves to the fact that poor Sasha was happier after all devoting himself to his Malmaison carnations and the manageable world of the green-house.

Natasha thought Sasha was lovable but insipid and Peter, her younger brother, charming but weak; her sisters were 'all good women, but none of them brilliant'. The tall and elegant Sonia, with her chestnut hair, was a bit of a flirt before marriage and then too austere and serious-minded afterwards; Sophia likewise was too earnest; Maria a bit of an invalid; poor Vera 'very high strung' and the man she married, the worthy Baron Offenberg, a most dreadful bore. Natasha was as blunt as her mother in her estimation of the faults of her kin.

The winters of Natasha's childhood were spent in the Mest-chersky house opposite the yellow and white buildings of Moscow University, just behind the Kremlin on the Nikitskaya. The summers, from late May until the end of September, were spent at Doughino.

I take out Baedeker's guide to the Russian Empire, 1914 edition, and follow the railway lines 200 miles west from Moscow to the province of Smolensk and find the river Vasousa. The river flowed through the bottom of the estate. In spring it would burst its banks and the surrounding countryside would be flooded, with clumps of trees marooned in the sodden fields. When the Mestcherskys arrived from Moscow in these wet springs to begin their summer at the estate, they would have to be poled through the fields by their servants in flat-bottomed boats from the station. Carriages would be waiting on the high ground to take them up through the white-columned gates past the twin spires of the family chapel to the house on the hill.

It was a peach-coloured two-storey eighteenth-century mansion, garlanded with vines, with six huge marble columns supporting a classical Corinthian portico. Hothouse plants decorated the balconies over the entrance and there were two life-size marble lions on either side of the doorway. In the photographs I count thirty-four windows looking out onto the English garden. There were a hundred rooms, stables, greenhouses and acres of park laid out in boxwood, pines and floral beds; the sloping meadows down to the river at the foot of the garden used to burst with flowers in the spring. Wherever she was afterwards, Natasha could always guide her mind's eye through the vanished rooms, along the big entrance hall lined with oak benches, up the two flights of stairs, past the illustrations from La Fontaine's fables in the gilt frames, through her father's study, to the dancing hall, the dining room furnished in maplewood, past the china cabinets, to her mother's boudoir. There her memory moved to a portrait of her grandmother in a dark-brown velvet dress with frills, her sparkling eyes as brown as the wood of the frame.

Somewhere behind, there was a door to the library. All along the rows of maplewood shelves were lined the books of her ancestor Nicholas Karamzin, flagged with his slips, scribbled over with his annotations. It was from this store of books that he had written his history of Russia. Through all the waystations of revolution and exile, Natasha was to insist on carrying the full three volumes of Karamzin's history of Alexander I's reign, in their red leather bindings decorated with the family crest. Like her mother's basin and ewer, these volumes were her talismans:

she held on to them to keep faith with all the other things she had left behind.

Above the library, there was a small theatre under the eaves, where the children gave performances in the summer for their parents and guests. They were excused lessons for rehearsals. The hairdresser from the local town came on the day of the performance to make the children up. Everyone from the surrounding villages came and the servants watched from the doorway. Vera and Natasha sat very still in their costumes, while the hairdresser wet his finger with his tongue, dipped it in the pot of rouge and dabbed pink on their cheeks. In the candlelit mirror they watched themselves becoming women.

I search the photographs of Doughino, prowl through the rooms with my magnifying glass. The parquet gleams in the light; a shadow cast by the curtained light from the windows streams across a room. In the corners, floor-to-ceiling Dutch stoves; against the walls, white alabaster statues of the Panins, furniture of the reign of Alexander I, curved armchairs made for leaning back in a tight uniform while playing whist. I see the reflection of a white Corinthian column in the sheen of a mahogany table. At the end of a corridor, a door has been left ajar. In the conservatory, papers have been left on the writing table. A quill pen lies on top of a newspaper on an escritoire. A card table awaits a game of whist after supper. The walls are crowded with portraits of ancestors: the paintings tilt away from the walls, leaving triangles of black shadow behind them. A chandelier hangs from the painted ceiling. Squares of light from the windows slant across the shiny rectangular inlay of the parquet.

In a photo of the conservatory at the edge of the focus I find a statue of Nikita Panin seated in a chair – like Houdon's study of Voltaire – a plump sombre man in a wig, with his legs crossed, one hand gripping the arm of the chair, the other resting on a folder of papers of state. He wears a star-shaped decoration on a sash around his chest. There is a sealed letter sculpted in bronze at his feet, and underneath the chair a pile of books. For someone sculpted at the height of his success, the expression on his worn face is oddly wistful.

His great-great-granddaughter Natasha grew up playing at his feet. The children were all told that if their games got too noisy, he would come down off his chair and kick their backsides with his buckled shoe. Later when they became teenagers, they were told about his moment of disgrace in the Empress's boudoir. Catherine the Great, aged by lust and power, spent hours making herself up in the boudoir. The chancellor, no longer a young man himself, became drowsy in that close, candlelit world of female odours. When at last the Empress strode out from behind the painted Japanese screen, her garter sash of power across her bosom, her cheeks daubed with paint, her eyes waxed with liner, she found her chancellor slumped in his chair asleep. It was one thing to argue with her about affairs of state; quite another to appear insensible to her charms. The family story was that she shook him awake and packed him off to his estates in disgrace.

The old bronze chancellor, wistful and disillusioned, always frightened Natasha when she went into the conservatory at night or passed the conservatory windows when she walked in the gardens on her way to bed. The candles cast their gleam over the fingers gripping the arm of the chair and there were dark shadows in the sockets of his unseeing eyes. She would pull her shawl closer and climb the stairs to her room, feeling the statue's gaze upon her back.

On fair mornings at eleven Fidki the Cossack would wheel Natasha's mother in a wicker Bath chair through the gravel pathways of the parks and gardens. The gardener would lean forward to hear her orders, and *Hofmeister* Bertram the forester would also make an appearance. The Bertrams had served the family as far back as the old Count himself. Brought from Germany in the 1780s to bring European order to the Count's Russian woods, father and son had succeeded each other, serving as both doctor to the trees and doctor to the family. When Natasha's mother called out the *Hofmeister* at night for the children's fevers, they would hear him stumping up the stairs damning *'diese verfluchte Familie'* – this accursed family – under his breath. Then he would be at their cots, bending over them and smelling of evergreen.

Gardening was her mother's passion, and the morning meetings with the *Hofmeister* and the gardener were as serious as a staff conference of generals. Natasha's mother would wave her stick about and the *Hofmeister* would grunt and bend over and look in the direction she was pointing. The new redwoods from California were to go there, there was to be a new alley of roses here, and what on earth were those dandelions doing on the English lawn? So seriously did she take her gardening that when her older son Sasha – in his only known gesture of defiance – said that when the estate was his he would like to cut down her favourite alley of cypresses, she disinherited him on the spot. The matter might have ended tragically. He spent weeks pleading with her that he had only been joking.

Natasha loved these tours of the garden with her mother, particularly the visit to the greenhouses: vast airy sheds with warm red earth underfoot and blowsy female statuary in the alcoves. In winter, the greenhouses were a lush corner of Crimea in northern Russia. Outside the lawns and the trees were draped with snow; inside, peaches and lemons ripened, warm to her touch.

Between Natasha and her mother there was a screen of nurses, butlers, tutors and gardeners, and older brothers and sisters. Natasha always held back; only when the others had left to start their own families did she find her way to her mother's heart. She remembered herself as being painfully shy; 'when scarcely out of baby age when meeting strangers I put up my arm to hide my face to the great indignation particularly of my eldest sister who assured me it was an affectation.' Her shyness, she always said, was her great misfortune. Nonsense, said her aunt, your shyness shows your great self-love and pride. If you would realize once and for all you are not even noticed or looked upon all that shyness would be gone. But she could not help it. She hid behind the curtains watching the others play.

The last of the litter, the gawky awkward one, Natasha clung to her older sister, the elegant Sonia, and used to weep when she disappeared to the society balls in Moscow, grazing her little sister with a fragrant kiss. Her sisters crossed the divide into the world of stays and button shoes, corsages and women's problems and left her behind in girlhood. Natasha sat in their boudoirs while they dressed at night and then would be left upstairs, sitting on the topmost step, hidden from view, watching the dancers whirl by the open door of the downstairs dining room. Later, when she was older, while her sisters danced the polka and the quadrille, and the *dirigeur*, the leader of the dance, would bring them a succession of young officers as partners, she played the *bouquetière*, the flower girl, wheeling a small cart of posies around the dance floor, stopping before each table so that the officers could offer their ladies a bouquet. A picture was taken of Natasha standing before her cart in her green pinafore, with a pink cap with ribbons in her curls – and then they packed her up to bed, while the dances surged beneath her in the bright rooms below.

Most of the winter months of her childhood were spent within sight of the Kremlin wall in Moscow in a large house with several adjoining buildings in Nikitskaya opposite the yellow and cream classical porticoes and domes of the university. In the faded photographs, there is an inner garden, laid down in grass, bisected by gravel pathways and on all sides the house rises around it, with awnings over the windows. In the gravel driveway outside a coachman in a full-length cream coat and a top hat sits on his box in the family brougham, holding on to the reins of a piebald mare. He is waiting for his master who is about to appear. The butler stands ready to open the door.

On the nights when all the lamps were lit and guests were expected for dinner, Natasha and Vera would slide down the banisters to the front door and ring the bell which the footman used to announce the arrival of visitors. Her father would appear at the head of the stairs and she and Vera would jump out to surprise him. Just before the visitors would arrive, the butler would go round the rooms with a long censer held on a stick. In the censer was a hot iron plate over which the butler would pour a perfume called Court Water. The sweet humid odour slipped along the hallways, under the doors, into the rooms and suffused the sheets on the beds. It would still be there, a fragrant ghost, when she tucked herself into bed.

On Easter Saturday night Natasha would sit in her best dress at the open window waiting for the Kremlin bells to sound. All day the cooks had been making *koulitch* and *paska* and the house smelled of sweet dough, raisins and almonds. By early evening, the Easter feast was ready in the dining room: the white dome of the *paska* stood in the centre of the long trestle table; there were bowls full of the dyed eggs with 'XB' – for 'Christ is Risen' – on each of them; and she had stained her hands green and blue from dipping the eggs in the dye in the pantry with her sister. At midnight the Kremlin bells would begin to boom out through the night air and the tolling and pealing would be taken up by church bells all around her, the white domed church at the top of the street where Pushkin had got married, the red brick one down the alley, the chapels in all the side streets, the sound rising to a crescendo of celebration. Then she would leap down from the window casement and run to the family chapel on the third floor where the choir – nuns from a neighbouring convent, house servants, soloists from the Choudofskoy choir – and her older sisters were already singing. The butler came up the stairs spreading the Court Water and calling out on each floor, 'Service is commencing,' and the servants and governesses and sisters and brothers would rush to take their places. Behind the butler came the priest and his acolytes in a procession up the winding red-carpeted stairs. And when the clergy in their white robes had exclaimed, 'Christ is risen, Christ is risen indeed,' and everyone in the chapel had lit their candles and embraced each other three times, they went out in the dawn air, to feel the breath of spring and the promise of resurrection from winter. And then they were back inside the dining room to feast on *paska* and *koulitch* and taste the abundance of the Easter feast after the fasting of Lent.

There were always jokes at the dinner table in the Moscow house. One which she was to tell her children was about the gentleman who peed in his top hat in a railway compartment, emptied it out of the window, bowed stiffly to the ladies present, placed the top hat back on his head and sat down in the seat opposite and resumed reading his newspaper. Minutes later, he unwrapped a cigar and, after bowing to the ladies, asked if he had their permission to smoke. When one of them replied that he had not bothered to ask their permission on a previous occasion, the gentleman replied, '*Ah, madame, ça c'était la nécessité, mais ceci*' – pointing to the cigar – '*c'est le plaisir.*'

There was another one about the old priest who had to marry an exceedingly ugly couple and who when the time came to give a homily could only grumble in French: '*Aimez-vous l'un l'autre, parce que si non, que Diable vous aimera.*'

The most reliable object of family jokes was the boys' tutor, Mr Bachinsky, who was a Pole and spoke Russian badly. When he wanted to tell Natasha's mother how close he felt to her, he said with a thick accent, 'I feel myself with you, Princess, as if in my own shirt.' Natasha and Vera continually teased Mr Bachinsky that he was getting old and must get married or he would be lonely. They would force him down on one knee in front of them, put his hand on his heart and make him practise his speech of proposal. He blushed marvellously.

Poor Mr Bachinsky. He was not only the boys' tutor, but also in charge of the family finances. He came to believe economies were called for. So an estate in the southern province of Voronezh was sold at a swindler's price. Mr Bachinsky was so distressed at being swindled that he returned to Poland. There he fell into a garden well and drowned.

Years later, Natasha would say to her sons, '*Racontez-moi*

quelque chose,' when they came back to her from far away. Tell me a story. She loved a story, the more 'far-fetched' the better and when it amused her, she would put her hands to her face and laugh soundlessly, rocking back and forth.

Peter, her youngest brother, was a 'specialist of silly inventions, an insipid fellow, really' – she couldn't understand what the girls saw in him – but he knew how to make her laugh. She would sit with him late at night when he was on leave from his cavalry regiment and listen to his stories while he polished his riding boots. He would start some long tale about his fiancée's family and get her laughing so hard that he would have to carry her upstairs to bed.

She was happiest in early childhood when her brothers and sisters were all still at home and she could run in their wake. At her 'buckfish changing age' – that phrase of hers for puberty – she stopped eating and began to fade away in mute resistance before the onset of womanhood. The professors were called, one so eminent he sent along an assistant beforehand to test the chairs he was to sit on. The professors prescribed the Riviera and she was despatched with her mother to the Grand Hotel Cannet in Cannes, where a lugubrious Baltic woman made her fatten up on *poudre de viandes* sandwiches. The French doctors were less deferential: a spoiled child, said Professor Cazalis of Nice; he packed her off to Aix les Bains. Water cures, eating cures, rest cures – she slipped into that archipelago of white hotels and sanatoria where some of her class seemed to spend their entire lives. When she came out she had recovered her appetite, but there remained a memory of the escape that could be hers if she just stopped eating. As the last one to leave home, the daughter most subjugated to her mother's love, she was also the daughter for whom the passage to womanhood was most regretfully embarked upon.

When Natasha was sixteen she spent her first winter in Nice with the family. She took her father's arm on the Promenade des Anglais during Carnival Week in February and they walked

[33]

through the crowds, ducking the showers of confetti, watching the clowns, joining in the singing and then escaping the crowds to stand at the end of the promenade alone together to watch the black calm of the winter sea.

She was in Nice with her mother in the winter of 1894 when *Hofmeister* Bertram wired them to come home to Doughino immediately. The master was ill. She raced back through Paris and Dresden and Berlin to find her father twisting and turning on his bed in the last stages of a fatal urinary and kidney infection. Surgeons and nurses were brought from Moscow to the estate. They slept on divans outside his room and the daughters took shifts sitting with him. She had the night watch. Just before morning, after weeks of suffering, he seemed to awake and to look about. Before she had time to call her mother in the next room, he looked up at his daughter and closed his eyes for ever.

The body was dressed and placed in a coffin on the billiard table in the conservatory. The daughters took turns keeping the vigil and reading psalms in the days and nights before the funeral. Natasha sat by the coffin through one night watch reading psalms from the Bible on her knees:

> I call to remembrance my song in the night.
> I commune with mine own heart.
> Will the Lord cast me off for ever?
> Hath God forgotten to be gracious?

Through the long hours of that night, as she sat and watched the sere and sunken face of her father, a curtain billowed in the draught, the wax from the candles dripped on the floor and the leaves of the palms scraped and shuffled against each other. She was seventeen years old.

After they buried him in the family crypt among the birch trees at Doughino, it was to Natasha that her mother turned in her grief. She insisted on being taken up to the attic and Natasha would sit on the boxes and watch her bent, beloved back as she rummaged frantically, pointlessly through deeds and old papers, trying to give the air that she could cope now that she was alone. It was a shock to discover this commanding woman so vulnerable now that the man she had dominated was gone. And there was the shock too of seeing her mother, for the first time, as an old woman. Years later Natasha wrote, 'It made my heart burst and I shed many tears alone. It seems being an old woman myself now, that since my childhood I have dreaded old age, and that old people have always made a heartrending impression upon me. It seems so tragic to notice the change in one's loved ones coming on. I am old myself now, but I feel I will never get over that feeling of awe and dread of old age.' Natasha was sixty-six when she wrote those lines, coming back full circle to the lonely daughter who watched her mother brought low by widowhood and sorrow.

All her sisters and brothers had begun their adult lives by then: Sasha had been sent to the lyceum and then to university, Peter to the regiment and the daughters to marriage: Natasha was at all family conferences when her sisters' suitors were mercilessly discussed and their antecedents checked, through the *Almanach de Gotha*. She was at the engagement parties, raised her champagne glass to their happiness, buttoned them into their wedding dresses, held their bouquets at the step of the landau and waved them down the long driveway to their honeymoons. And then she was left alone with her mother, the aging autocrat in the Bath chair. Natasha became the dutiful daughter, reading Carlyle's *History of Frederick the Great* to her in the long summer afternoons; the one who pushed her Bath chair along the Promenade des Anglais in the weak winter light and who, when they were back at Doughino, accompanied her on the daily tour of the estate gardens, watching the old hands palpating the peaches in the greenhouse and tapping her beloved evergreens with her stick. When her mother complained of the cold, Fidki, the lazy Cossack, would turn the Bath chair on the gravel and wheel her back home and Natasha would follow behind.

She slept in the next room to her mother, ready to rise, to comfort, to listen to the groans and lamentations. There was a pain in the old woman's breast which would not go away. The quacks descended: one whose name was Blitz prescribed massage, but the pain grew worse and the lump in her breast began to swell. Finally it became impossible to deny what was happening. From Doughino, a wire was sent to a surgeon in Moscow. He arrived by train seven hours later, took one look at his patient and ordered that a mass be sung in the chapel and that a room be scrubbed down for an operation.

Her mother's oldest friend, Countess Sheremetieff, who had been a nurse in the Russo-Turkish War, held her head while the chloroformed gauze was passed over her face. Under the chloroform, Natasha's mother shouted frantically that the surgeon should give up medicine and become a teacher, where he could at least do humanity some good, instead of inflicting such torture. Natasha waited in the chloroform-filled passageway, saying her prayers, listening to her mother's babbling in the next room.

The operation bought them all several years' respite. Life resumed at Doughino: the peasant children brought berries to the pantry door and the cook bought them to make jam. In the early autumn, there were mushroom hunts with the peasant children in the damp piney places under the trees and the cook would bake them into mushroom pies. In the spring, they would make a drink from the sap of birch trees and another with new buds of blackcurrant, flavoured with lemons and oranges, sugar and champagne. There were troika rides in summer, sleigh rides in the winter, muffled deep in furs. On the long summer afternoons, Natasha would take her nephews and nieces down to the meadow by the river while her sisters slept with their husbands upstairs in the bedrooms darkened against the heat.

The old woman's rule was drawing to a close but none of her daughters or sons-in-law dared disobey her. From June till September, she insisted the clan must be about her though she did not actually like to see them once they were there. On her morning walk, she forbade the sight of her grandchildren and if they heard the Bath chair crunching along the gravel they would scurry for cover behind the box hedges until the procession had gone by.

Doughino was a closed universe with the world held at a distance beyond the white gates. When the jangling bells of troikas were heard approaching in the park, Natasha and the servants would come running to see who the visitors might be. There was Chomiakoff, after 1905 one of the presidents of the Duma, a 'queer man', Mongolian in appearance, always contradicting himself; and the elegant Ourousoffs, as delicate as moths, in their fawn riding clothes, recounting the latest gossip from the Riviera in a Russian flavoured with a slight French accent. She remembered best Professor Rachinsky, an excitable little man, with a face like a squeezed-out lemon, yellow but full of life. An indefatigable eccentric, he arrived with tremendous bustle from his estate in Tver province and seemed to inspect every leaf in the garden, and quizzed the village priest about the state of the peasants' moral education. At his own estate, he ran a school for peasant children.

Natasha wondered whether Professor Rachinsky's philanthropy ever came to anything – one of his peasant children became a priest, another became an artist – but the rest returned to the soil, untouched by the Professor's lessons. She was generous enough herself, as her father had been, but she was unburdened by that Tolstoyan sense of guilt and responsibility for the peasants that drove the old Professor on his grinding round of benevolence.

There was another visitor who talked like Rachinsky, a typical Russian madcap of a doctor, who had handsome red hair and who used to sit and spill out all his Tolstoyan theories to Natasha after dinner in the study. She was attracted to him, though marriage with a young country doctor was out of the question, and she liked the look of Russian absorption which came over him when he talked of putting the country to rights. He told her that he liked her austerity, the plain black dresses, the simple unadorned meals at table, the frugality observed in this most splendid of old houses. He said it would prepare her well for whatever life had to offer. She found the compliment amusing: it was said so sombrely, as if darkness lay ahead for both of them.

The subject of the peasantry always seemed to send the men at Doughino into that special mood of earnest self-importance which came over aristocratic Russians when they discussed a 'social question'. She herself had very few thoughts about the peasants. They were in another world beyond the gates. Only one photograph in her family album shows peasants in the frame. The picture was taken sometime in the 1890s at the festival of St Peter and St Paul by the doorway of the family chapel at Doughino. Women in white kerchiefs crowd around the icons which are draped in white and carried by deacons with flowing black hair and vestments. The sea of faces is turned towards the icons, but one face – that of a woman in a white kerchief – is looking over her shoulder. Her back is broad and strong; there is an apron around her waist. She is staring at someone 'from the big house', and her gaze is curious and unafraid.

In just twenty years these peasants were to burn Doughino to the ground and make the owner, mild stooping Sasha, sweep out the latrines in the prison yard at Sichevka. This irony – that I know what is coming and Natasha could not – is one of the barriers between us. I have to forget what comes next. To share her past, I have to forget her future.

But so did she. How, for example, was she to preserve the original colour of her memories of the Coronation ceremonies of 1896 from the wash of retrospective foreboding that swept over all recollections of Nicholas and Alexandra after 1917? She was watching from the stands outside the cathedral in Moscow as the imperial couple arrived and she believed afterwards that she had felt a chill of anxiety when she saw the Tsarina descend from the coach, with her stiff, strained expression, holding on tight to the arm of her tragic-eyed consort. As the Tsarina passed their stand, bowing to right and left at the old families, Natasha and her mother noticed that the young queen's arms and face were discoloured by red flushes, a nervous symptom, the insignia of dread.

This was one of exile's subtler wounds – the way time future recoloured time past, so that sitting by the window in the Quebec countryside she could not help feeling that her entire past was leading to her dispossession. Each memory, even the blushes on the Tsarina's arms, was dispossessed of its innocent opacity, its plurality of possible meanings and made to follow time's fatal vector. Recollection for her was not only an escape from the diminishing circle of old age, but also a struggle to escape the future's grip on the past. When she stared out of the window at the snow of a foreign land and fought to remember the name of the gardeners at Doughino or the word for a type of Turkish delight made from berries, she was fighting to save her past from the pall of inevitability that the future cast back upon it like a malign shadow.

THREE
FATHER AND SON

====

One of my grandfather Paul's earliest memories was of Sundays at his grandfather Ignatieff's house on Gagarinsky Prospekt in St Petersburg in 1879. Paul was nine years old and he came with his father and mother, his four brothers and two sisters to attend the Sunday service at the family chapel. The chapel was full of uncles, aunts, cousins and relatives: the Zouroffs, Engalicheffs and Maltsevs. At the back stood the housemaids, porters, coachmen and butlers led by the chief servant, Vassily, serf since boyhood to the master.

At the front stood the patriarch of the family, Paul's namesake, Count Paul Ignatieff, State Councillor, Chairman of His Majesty's Council of Ministers, Protector of the Russian Throne during His Majesty's absences on the field of battle against the Turks. Count Paul Ignatieff was by then nearly eighty, loaded with infirmities and honours, leaning on the arm of his wife, Countess Maria. His sons and their families stood behind him. Of these sons, the oldest was Count Nicholas, my grandfather Paul's father. Paul stood next to his father, and they sang together, bass and soprano entwining. They knelt together, Paul in his sailor suit, his father in a general's uniform and high leather boots. They said their prayers and at the end of the service everyone approached the altar in strict order of family precedence to kiss the cross. Then Count Paul and Countess Maria stiffly turned and led the family procession in to Sunday lunch.

In the dining room, the table was set for thirty. Each went to his appointed place, the children shooed to their chairs by their

mothers. They all stood waiting until grandfather and grandmother were helped into their places at opposite ends of the table.
Count Paul said a blessing and then the family babble started.
Paul told his Zouroff cousins about Countess Tiesenhausen's
monkey, how that summer in the Crimea it leaped from its perch
in the tree onto his shoulders, with the chain on its ankle jangling
and spinning, how it tickled his hair with its fingers.

No wine was served at lunch – Paul's grandfather did not allow
cards or spirits in the house – and the food was plain soldiers'
food, easy on an old man's digestion, soup and *kotleti*, breaded
cutlets of chicken. Paul waited for the *kissail*, the dessert of
whipped cranberries with the sweet metallic taste.

Grandfather Paul who now broke his bread with shaking hands
once held his regimental colours aloft on the Champs Elysées
when, having driven Napoleon from Russia, the Preobrajensky
Guards rode into Paris in 1815. He had been seventeen then, an
ensign in the Household Company and only son of a forgotten
fort commander on the Polish frontier. He belonged to that
generation of young officers who returned from the campaign
against Napoleon to Russian barrack towns dreaming of Paris,
talking of Liberty, that generation who were to lead the December uprising against Tsar Nicholas I in 1825. Many of his fellow
officers in the cafés and billiard halls, the regimental dances and
parade grounds, became Decembrists, but he promised his
mother he would be sensible. On that December morning in
1825, the young Tsar looked anxiously from his balcony window
overlooking Winter Palace Square for detachments to come to
his support to quell the revolt stirring through the regimental
barracks. The first platoons to stream beneath the arches and
take up position were commanded by Captain Paul Ignatieff.

While his Decembrist friends paid for their dreams in Siberia,
Paul Ignatieff was showered with the Tsar's favour. Appointed
aide-de-camp at twenty-eight, by his early thirties he was already
commander of the Corps des Pages and in this post he remained
for twenty-five years, the schoolmaster to two generations of the

Russian military elite. He had former pupils in every ministry, in every corridor of the Winter Palace. By 1861, Paul Ignatieff had been appointed governor of Petersburg. It was he who ordered the Cossack detachments to charge down the Nevsky Prospekt to scatter the first student demonstrations against Tsar Alexander II with the flats of their sabres. It was Paul Ignatieff who ordered the imprisonment of hundreds – including the young Fyodor Dostoevsky – and the expulsions from the university of thousands more. In exile in London, the Russian essayist Alexander Herzen wrote of the February repression: 'Give ear, for even darkness does not prevent you from listening, from all corners of our enormous land, from the Don and the Ural, from the Volga and the Dnieper, a moan is growing. This is the first roar of the sea billow which begins to rage.'

As far as Paul Ignatieff was concerned, Herzen wrote nonsense: there was no gathering storm, just a lot of spoiled and disobedient students who needed to be taught a lesson. He was a scholarly general, who knew his Latin and his Greek, a man of few words, sober, circumspect and watchful. After choosing to serve the Tsar against his Decembrist friends, he found the groove of power and followed it steadily, serving both Tsars, Nicholas I and the emancipator of the serfs, Alexander II. He was a sturdy and unquestioning bulwark of autocracy to whom the Tsar turned in the 1870s when he was looking for an unadventurously reliable chairman for his Council of Ministers.

Paul Ignatieff's first son – Nicholas – was born in 1832. The future Tsar Alexander II attended his christening and stood by the baptismal font. Educated at the Corps des Pages, and then made aide-de-camp of the Tsar, Nicholas was in his twenties during the Crimean War. Instead of winning glory at Inkerman or Sebastopol, he had to content himself with comic-opera service on board the first Russian submarine, a clumsy wood and iron experiment that capsized and threw him into the Baltic on its first trial. At twenty-three he was sent as military attaché to London, where the British Foreign Office found him a 'clever, wily fellow'.

In London he deepened his already profound hostility to British foreign policy.

Nicholas was only twenty-six when in 1858 he was despatched by the Tsar to central Asia to negotiate a trade treaty with the khans and emirs of Bokhara and Khiva. It was a two-month journey by horse and camel south and east from Orenberg, the southernmost border town of the Russian Empire, across the Barsak sands and around the northern shores of the Caspian Sea. The worst of the journey was the boat ride up the Oxus River, terrible days being dragged through the winding miles of reeds by Khivan boatmen, lying in the bottom stripped to the waist, tormented by thirst and flies. When Ignatieff and his party finally reached the red adobe palaces of Bokhara, standing in the dusty marketplace filled with filthy children, veiled women and traders with gold teeth, the pathway to the Khan's tent was flanked by blackened heads on pikes, trophies of justice and revenge. Ignatieff sat cross-legged on the carpets of the Emir, drinking tea, exchanging gifts, and learning the patience and ruthlessness of his hosts. There seemed some affinity between the Russian envoy and the Asian prince, some Tartar filiation in the hooded eyes, black moustaches, and the mixture of bravery and cunning. Before he departed he and the Emir had signed a treaty giving Russia free navigation of the Oxus for her steamers in the Aral Sea, reduction of tariffs on Russian caravans and liberation of Russians held captive by the Emir.

Ignatieff and his Cossacks set out for home in the blizzards of November, and when they stumbled back into Fort Number One at the southernmost Russian border in mid-December, they were wearing Khivan yashmaks over their lice-infested uniforms and their faces were burned black from the winter wind. They hastened to the first chapel and fell down on their knees.

The Khivan and Bokharan expedition made Nicholas a Petersburg celebrity, one of the builders of empire in Asia. Within a year, still only twenty-seven, he set off from Petersburg with a Cossack detachment and an ammunition train bound for

Peking. Changing sleighs and coaches at every inn, fording the Siberian rivers on the spring ice and then forging ahead on horseback across the Mongolian plains, he had soon left his baggage train and ammunition wagons far behind. In May, as the cherry blossoms shivered in the wind, he rode through the gates of the Forbidden City, unkempt, unshaven and travel-worn, watched on every side by silent Chinese.

He arrived at a decisive moment in the plunder of the Celestial Empire by the Great Powers. A British and French fleet, loaded with a landing force, were cruising up and down within sight of Shanghai. When he offered his services to the Chinese Emperor as a negotiator between the Chinese and their foreign enemies, the Chinese Emperor had him placed under house arrest. To escape, he got his valet to saw half way through the axle of his carriage and then they rode together into the middle of the main gate out of the Forbidden City. There the valet jumped on the axle to break it and they both leaped onto the coach horses and rode off to Shanghai, leaving the Chinese piled up behind the broken carriage. In Shanghai, he made contact with the British and French fleets, promised Russia's neutrality, and then sat peacefully on the deck of a Russian cruiser in the Yellow Sea while the British and French landed and marched on Peking. When the Europeans had the Forbidden City encircled, he renewed his offer of mediation to the Emperor and the Europeans, and this time it was accepted. By his negotiations, the Manchu dynasty and the Imperial City were saved from the sack, while the Europeans were granted the trading concessions they had sought. The negotiator then presented his bill for his services: definitive cession to Russia of the territory north of the Amur and east of the Ussuri. With this treaty in his pocket, Ignatieff and his Cossacks saddled up for Petersburg on 13 November 1860. Anxious that the Great Powers would bring pressure to bear on the Tsar to undo his work, Nicholas raced home across the snows of Asia to defend his treaty in person. When he arrived in Irkutsk in early December, the governor general of Siberia, Count Muraviev, ordered a street renamed in his honour and one of Muraviev's clerks, a bear-like political prisoner called Mikhail Bakunin, wrote a marvelling letter to Alexander Herzen saying he had just met a young Russian colonel who was the only living man in Russia: 'He does not reason, he writes little, but, a rare thing in Russia, he *acts*.'

On 1 January 1861, rimed in ice, tottering with exhaustion, Nicholas Ignatieff stood in his father's house, having traversed the whole of Asia on horseback in six weeks. He backed away from his mother's embraces: his floor-length travelling coat was stiff with ice on the outside, swarming with fleas on the inside. Vassily took it off his back and sent it downstairs to be burned. The young master then subsided into a hot bath. Next morning he was received by the Tsar, decorated with the Order of St Vladimir, promoted to general and shortly thereafter made head of the Asian department of the Foreign Office. Without firing a shot, he had secured for Russia a wild terrain the size of France and Germany combined and the hinterland of Vladivostok, the new empire's port on the Pacific.

In June 1861, in the German spa town of Wiesbaden, General Nicholas Ignatieff, then twenty-nine, married Princess Ekaterina Galitzine, one of the beauties of her day, and great-granddaughter of Field Marshal Kutuzov, commander of the Russian armies in the War of 1812. She was nineteen, with a high forehead, black hair, large brown eyes and a very charming slightly dimpled upper lip. She was my grandfather Paul's mother. At the Sunday dinners at the Ignatieffs' house on the Gagarinsky Prospekt, she was nearly forty, mother of three boys, two girls and already expecting another child. One of her particular gestures was to crack a walnut between her teeth. She did so now and handed a kernel to her son Paul, while dabbing at his sailor's suit with her napkin to remove a splash of cranberry dessert.

At the end of Sunday lunch, everyone stood and Vassily helped old Count Paul to his feet: the grandchildren approached to kiss him on both cheeks and to receive a pat on their head. Young Paul watched his grandfather disappear down the long hallway on Vassily's arm, his old black boots squeaking on the wood, his bent silhouette framed for a second by the grey light streaming through the Neva-facing windows. The walnut doors closed behind his grandfather. The old man who had carried his regiment's flag down the Champs Elysées in 1815 sank into sleep on the divan in his study. Vassily guarded his peace in a chair by the door. It was the last time Paul was ever to see his grandfather. The Count died the following year and these ritual Sundays were to be no more.

*

My grandfather Paul was born in August 1870 in the cream-coloured summer house of the Russian ambassador in Constantinople, high on a cliff overlooking the Bosphorus. I have a photograph of him at his mother's feet, taken by a society photographer when he was just two years old. He is wearing flounced skirts, high button shoes and a little sash around his waist. His blond hair has been slicked down for the photograph. His mother is wearing a grand dark dress, a diaphanous curve of tulle and crepe, and she leans over him, her hand grazing the back of his head. He has inherited the pucker of her upper lip, and his gaze, like hers, shrinks back from this public sharing of the closed circle of their devotion. All his life, in moments of distress, he was to return to this serene presence whose dark skirts enfold his tiny shape and whose hand grazes the top of his head.

In his early childhood, she was more absent than present, an ambassador's wife with official duties and a huge establishment to run, who left the children to the nursemaids, and who would lean over his cot to give him a goodnight kiss. If he crept down the hall to the top of the landing, he could see her in the great hall below, receiving guests beside his father in his dress uniform, flanked by Bosnian and Montenegran doorkeepers with their hooked knives.

Paul's father Nicholas, a tall heavy-set man with drooping brown moustaches and a round domed forehead, was now Russian ambassador to the court of the Turkish Sultan. As such he was also defender of the Orthodox minorities under Ottoman rule, intriguer and fomenter of every revolt in that senescent empire and master of a tentacular network of Bulgarian, Bosnian, Rumanian, Turkish and Cretan informers. His sons could watch him from the nursery window in the embassy garden, strolling up and down the alleys of azaleas, hands behind his back deep in thought, as men with thick black beards and moustaches, priests, fiacre drivers, seamen, chandlers – men of all descriptions – muttered their reports into his ear. They made him the best informed ambassador on the Bosphorus, the spider at the centre of the web, the master of all Balkan intrigues. The British ambassadors, Lord Lytton and his successor Henry Elliot, thought him a jocular and amusing mountebank, and the French ambassador referred to him as Mentir Pasha. But none of them was able to stop him from making Russia the dominant power in the Balkans. At the Constantinople Conference of 1877, as Turkey and Russia stood on the brink of war, Lord Salisbury teased him about his network of spies. Ignatieff replied that he had thousands of them: every Christian in the Balkans who had lost someone in the Turkish massacres was his voluntary informant. During the same conference, Salisbury watched with amazement while Ignatieff, thinking Salisbury's back was turned, erased and re-drew the proposed treaty boundaries to enlarge Russian gains in Bessarabia by several thousands of square miles. When Salisbury ventured to point out this legerdemain, Ignatieff smiled and shrugged his shoulders: '*Monsieur le Marquis est si fin, on ne peut rien lui cacher.*' Salisbury reported home to the British Cabinet that Ignatieff was a 'brilliant and fluent talker who adorns his conversations with fictions so audaciously unconvincing as to become a constant source of amusement'.

Salisbury did not make the mistake of underestimating his man: indeed he came under his spell. Ignatieff's temperament was a puzzling blend of theatrical bluff, blunt candour, high Slavic emotion and lawyerly cunning. When Ignatieff arrived in England in 1876, Salisbury invited him and his wife to Hatfield House for a country weekend, much to the irritation of Queen Victoria who believed that neither Salisbury nor her ambassador in Constantinople was doing enough to prevent the Russians from gaining control of the Dardanelles. When Disraeli reported back to the Queen about the Russians' weekend at Hatfield House, his note concentrated almost entirely on Countess Ignatieff: 'a great lady, pretty, and they say, very agreeable, except when he recommended to her some Apollinaris water. Not the custom of Russian ladies. When they offered her wine, sherry or Manzanilla, she always answered "Any one," but never took any one. But [she] is very calm and collected and must have therefore had an early training at it. The fine ladies who had heard that Madame Ignatieff was even finer than themselves and gave herself airs, determined not to yield without a struggle. Lady Londonderry staggered under the jewels of three united families.'

Back in Constantinople, she told her son Paul that Hatfield House had been a vast, cheerless place where at night, when they were about to retire, a retainer handed them a lighted candle at the foot of the stairs and left them to find their own way down the damp corridors to their frozen beds. England, she told her children, was a barbarous place compared to Russia.

By the mid-1870s, Paul's father was the most powerful figure on the Bosphorus, Sultan Abdul Aziz's main foreign confidant, while his mother was the cynosure of the diplomatic corps. At the embassy receptions, she wore a necklace made of dozens of turquoise stars encrusted with diamonds, a gift of the Sultan, and not a few foreign ambassadors admitted they were under her spell. Her husband charmed the Sultan, while fomenting revolt behind his back. He was not above using blackmail to attain his ends. Deft allusion to what his spies told him about the sexual tastes of the Sultan's brothers did much to make the Sultan pliable.

Ignatieff played the keyboard of the European press with the same cynical virtuosity, feeding both the pan-Slavist publicists at home and the Gladstonian liberals abroad with stories of Turkish atrocities against the Balkan Christians. A natural mimic, he put on English country heartiness for Russell of *The Times*, and his rolling French r's for the correspondent of *Le Figaro*. In 1876, he toured the capitals of Europe drumming up support for the Russian cause against the Turks. In London, the cartoonist Spy drew him for *Vanity Fair*, bringing out the long straight fleshy nose, the sandy moustache and the formidable curvature of his frock coat. 'A manipulator of phrases' was the caption in *Vanity Fair*.

In Berlin Bismarck came away pleasantly surprised from his meetings with the Russian ambassador. Ignatieff was less of a windbag and more of a force to be reckoned with than press reports had suggested. Ignatieff told Bismarck that he wanted to accomplish a Russian revenge for the humiliations of the Crimean War through diplomacy rather than through force of arms. The Ottoman Empire, he said, was an artichoke, whose leaves he would peel off at his leisure, one at a time.

As he progressed through Europe in 1876, giving interviews to the press, posing for cartoonists, holding talks with the great powers, his Foreign Minister in St Petersburg, Prince Gorchakov, grew more and more impatient. Ignatieff, after all, was his subordinate, and it was intolerable to hear him speaking for Russian interests abroad without bothering to consult the Ministry at home. Yet Gorchakov knew that for the moment Ignatieff was untouchable. His courtship of the Slavophile press had made him a national figure at home, and his father had sufficient influence with the Tsar to protect his son from any whispering campaign mounted against him by the Foreign Ministry.

Ignatieff was that anomaly: a diplomat with a policy of his own. But he was not an adventurer. He was shrewd enough to know that any false move in the Balkans could be catastrophic. He made it clear to the Christians of Bosnia, Serbia and Montenegro that he would support them only so long as their campaign against the Turks did not pitch the area into a European war. 'Never "try" anything,' he told his Christian spies. 'Leave it alone if you cannot see it through to the end, but once you put your hand to something, never yield.' This was his motto: to balance daring with care. In the upward spiral of Slav and Christian revolts, massacres and counter-massacres that brought Russia and Turkey to war in 1877, he played for time until the Russian army would be ready to deal the blow that his policy had striven to prepare.

When war came in 1877, his son Paul, then aged seven, was evacuated down the cliffs to the Bosphorus at night and rowed out to a paddle-steamer riding at anchor with its windows blacked out to elude the Turkish sentries. Next morning when he awoke the steamer was cutting through the Black Sea, taking the family to the safety of the Crimea. While the son played Turks and Russians with the peasant boys in the fields of the family estate at Kroupodernitsa in the Ukraine, the father rushed to join the Tsar's side in the muddy little Balkan towns that served as army headquarters. Before leaving for the front, the Tsar appointed Nicholas's father, the old general Paul Ignatieff, protector of the Russian throne in his absence.

Through the terrible months of the siege of Plevna, Nicholas Ignatieff stood by the Tsar's side while the monarch trained his field glasses on the agonizingly costly assaults by his troops on the Turkish redoubt. Once the siege was broken, he pleaded with the Tsar to take the campaign all the way to Constantinople, to make Russia at last master of the Dardanelles. Against him were ranged the Tsar's uncle, Grand Duke Nicholas, and in Petersburg, the Foreign Ministry, both of whom counselled a defensive strategy.

The Russo-Turkish War was the first campaign that Europe read about the next day in the telegraphed despatches of war correspondents at the front. Ignatieff became the Tsar's public-relations impresario, doling out morsels of hard information to the correspondents in return for access to the army telegraph and titbits of information of their own. At one point during the see-saw battle for the Shipka Pass, Ignatieff pulled the *Evening News* messenger off his horse and marched him into the Tsar's tent so that the blood-spattered boy could bring the monarch the latest state of the struggle in the passes.

After Plevna fell in the late autumn of 1877, the Russian armies began to pour through the ice-bound Balkan defiles towards Constantinople. Soon they were at the outskirts of the city. A British fleet was patrolling in the Dardanelles and a face-to-face encounter with the British Empire was only hours away. The Grand Duke called a halt and negotiated an armistice with the Turks. Hearing this news in Bucharest Ignatieff was beside himself at the thought that fifteen years of assiduous plotting on his part was about to be frustrated by timidity on the battlefield. He raced across the snow-bound passes to Russian headquarters. Once the sleigh overturned and pitched his papers and baggage into a ravine, but he scrambled out, mounted one of his guard's horses and raced on to Russian headquarters where, scarcely dismounted, he began dressing down the Grand Duke in front of the general staff. Eventually the Grand Duke exploded and said he was damned if Ignatieff was going to saddle Russia with a war against England. The Russian troops would stay where they were.

Instead of presiding over a conference to dismember the Ottoman Empire, Ignatieff was ordered to turn the armistice into a permanent peace. At San Stefano, a little town on the Sea of Marmara, between the Mediterranean and the Black Sea, he re-drew the map of the Ottoman Empire while the defeated Turks watched in disconsolate silence. Bessarabia, lost in the Crimean War, was returned to Russia. Bosnia, Serbia and Herzegovina were given their independence and a new state of Bulgaria, with frontiers that stretched to within miles of

Constantinople to the east and within miles of the Aegean on the south, was created as a client of the Russian Empire.

Scarcely had the treaty's terms been published than Bismarck in Berlin, Disraeli in London and Andrassy in Vienna set out to undo it, with the assistance of Gorchakov and the Russian Foreign Ministry in Petersburg. Disraeli considered that a client state of Russia with access to the Aegean and the Dardanelles was a threat to British sea-lanes; the Austro-Hungarians considered the independence of the new Balkan states a threat to their designs on domination of the Balkan peninsula and Bismarck said he could only permit the existence of the new Bulgaria if it was headed by a German prince. In Petersburg, the combined opposition of the Great Powers and his own Foreign Ministry was too much for the Tsar. He was persuaded that Ignatieff had gone too far.

The wheel of the ambassador's fortunes began to turn. In February 1878, the treaty of San Stefano made him a national hero; in April the Tsar ennobled the family; all male descendants of Paul Ignatieff were to take the title of Count. But in May, Count Nicholas found himself banished to his estates south of Kiev; in September, brooding on the front porch of the manor house at Kroupodernitsa, he read the telegraph reports from the conference in Berlin where his treaty was dismembered and everything he had striven to achieve for fifteen years was traded away. The boundaries of Bulgaria were driven back from the edge of Constantinople to the Shipka Pass in the north, and from the Aegean to the hinterlands of Macedonia. The howls of betrayal that issued from the Slavophile press throughout Russia were small comfort to his wounded vanity.

Gloomy and embittered, he took the whole family to Nice in the winter of 1878–79 to soak up the sun and to escape Petersburg. His son Paul remembered how miserably cold the Riviera was that winter: the olive logs burned fitfully in the grate, sending smoke throughout the corridors of their clammy villa. Outside the oranges in the groves wore little hats of snow. Paul tiptoed round the house while his father brooded and his mother rested upstairs: another child was due in June.

Then just as suddenly as it had vanished, his father's furious energy returned. He whisked them home again during the last week of Lent, with an addition to the troupe of nannies, valets, maids and coachmen that followed in their wake. This was a new tutor for Paul, Monsieur Castellot, a professor of mathematics at the Collège d'Etampes. He was a neat little man who always wore a frock coat, a top hat and the blue ribbon of his Palme Académique in his lapel.

The family party swept home across Europe via Florence and Vienna, switching from the train to carriages at a small station in the Ukraine. It was a grand procession, this homecoming, with four carriages, Paul's parents in the first, the boys and Monsieur Castellot in the second, the girls and their nurses in the third, and the rest of the servants in the fourth. They thundered along the dusty roads, with Monsieur Castellot up on the box beside the coachman, the tails of his frock coat folded over his knees and his mouth opening and closing in alarm as the coaches rumbled across the rough-hewn planks of the local bridges or, where there were no bridges, thrashed through the stream and up onto the meandering cart tracks which led through the fields to home.

They spent one night along the way at Porechie, an abandoned estate Paul's father was interested in buying. The old wooden veranda sagged, the windows were cobwebbed, and a steward showed them through the damp and peeling rooms, hastily pulling dust sheets off the furniture. Paul's father stretched out on a dusty sofa, pulled his greatcoat over his shoulders and announced that this was where they would bivouac for the night. His pregnant wife was bedded down on an old sofa and the boys were despatched next door with Monsieur Castellot. The steward spread hay on the floor for them to sleep on and Paul remembered that all night the boys shrieked and threw hay at each other, while Monsieur Castellot tried in vain to restore order, wondering all the while what could ever have possessed him to leave the Collège d'Etampes for this troupe of savages.

Next day, the coaches rolled through the gates of Kroupodernitsa, the family home in the rolling wheat and sugar-beet fields southwest of Kiev. It was not a grand estate: no imperial columns or neat English lawns, but instead a plain whitewashed Ukrainian house of three stories, with three wings, built by Paul's father sometime in the 1860s. There were Ukrainian fan decorations on the rooftops, carved wood fluting over the latticed shutters and inside, small chintzy rooms crammed with portraits of old ancestors and memorabilia from Peking, Khiva, Bokhara and Constantinople: silks and swords, muskets and wall hangings. The driveway was rough earth and the back gardens that ran down to the river Ross were a jungle of woods, cut through here and there by chestnut alleys. Peasant children were underfoot everywhere: queuing at the door of the pantry with berries for the cook to buy for jam or lining up outside the Countess's rooms to be treated with her homeopathic remedies for cuts and fevers. A short walk from the house was the church, a small-scale Santa Sofia built of brick overlooking the river, and around it clustered a raggle-taggle village of thatched whitewashed cottages.

Paul spent all his summers there and grew up a country child. The Ukrainian summers were dry and hot, scented with the strong odours of grain and manure from the surrounding fields. The still and airless afternoons were broken with screaming plunges into the river Ross. In the evenings the coachman and Monsieur Castellot would use him as a bird-dog on their hunting expeditions in the marshes. They would run him to exhaustion in search of game and then take turns carrying him home asleep in their arms.

When Paul was old enough to harness the pony and trap he would set out on the bright cool mornings and race through the oak woods to Bossibrod, the little wooden station built specially for the family on the Kiev–Odessa railway line. He would pick up his father's mail at the station and bowl along home with *Le Figaro*, *The Times* and *Novoe Vremie* from St Petersburg jouncing on the seat beside him. His father would be pacing the veranda in his dressing gown, sipping his coffee, waiting to pore over the papers for signs of the political climate back in Petersburg. He bore his banishment fretfully and longed for a return to power.

For several months in 1879 he was recalled, but only to serve as temporary governor for the annual commercial fair and market at Nizhni Novgorod. With his usual energy, he ordered the old *bidonville* of wooden and tin shacks that had served the market for centuries to be knocked down and replaced with vaulted steel and glass hangars of the kind he had seen in Les Halles in Paris. But this was not the work he longed for and he was soon back on the veranda in Kroupodernitsa, pacing and brooding and then making furious visitations to buy up vacant properties nearby. He plunged into speculation as he had once plunged into Asian adventure. Speculators came to him with propositions and he was soon deep in the Caspian caviar business and the Volga steamboat trade. His interest in these concerns was fitful and erratic and he turned them over to an ingratiating young steward, Grinevetsky. The family soon had its doubts about Grinevetsky, who was to be found living in the best hotel in Kiev, profiting from what he could skim off the Ignatieff enterprises. Nicholas's wife tried to get her husband to restrain his financial impulsiveness, but he never tolerated her interference. If they wouldn't let him serve his country, he grumbled, he could at least improve his neighbourhood. Dilapidated estates were purchased and done up, steamboats named after General Ignatieff began plying the Volga, and for the moment at least there was money enough to pay for this balm to wounded pride.

The call back to service in Petersburg finally came in March 1881, at a time of national crisis. Nicholas's old master, Alexander II, who had freed the serfs in 1861 and had triumphed over the Turks in 1878, was assassinated by terrorists in a Petersburg street. His successor, the massive and dim-witted Alexander III, began a search for men ruthless enough to put down what he believed was a conspiracy that threatened the future of the dynasty itself. The new Tsar had served at Plevna in the Turkish campaign and remembered late-night conversations with General Ignatieff in which he had asked for advice about his future reign and had been told with gruff decisiveness: 'Draw closer to the people.' Alexander III consulted his uncle the Grand Duke Nicholas and was told that Ignatieff was often a 'liar in small things', but might be truthful with big things. This equivocal recommendation was good enough for the new monarch. In May 1881, Ignatieff was named Minister of the Interior. All of the energies dammed up since San Stefano were now poured into the task of mastering the most serious crisis the autocracy had faced since the Decembrist uprising of 1825. He masterminded the arrest and deportation of agitators, the infiltration of émigré groups in Zürich and Paris and student clubs and salons at home. He reorganized the secret police, the Okhrana, and turned them loose on the People's Will, the terrorist group that had struck down Alexander II.

Ignatieff put his signature to the Law on Extraordinary and Temporary Measures, which gave provincial governors the power to suspend normal legal procedure and individual civil rights wherever a strike, an attack or a riot required it. The decree also empowered the government to hand suspects over to summary courts martial, to order house arrests and domestic searches, and to outlaw any meetings, close any institution, or suspend any newspaper as it saw fit. Until 1917, these measures were to remain the key statutes of the autocracy, its chief legal weapon in its losing struggle for survival. It was from their heavy hand that the young Lenin and Stalin were to acquire their contempt for legality and due process.

Ignatieff also balanced repression with reform. He agreed on a plan with the representatives of local government, the *zemstvos*, to reduce the head taxes and redemption payments which had burdened the peasantry since Emancipation and to establish an agricultural bank to assist wealthier peasants to consolidate their holdings.

As Minister of the Interior, he was in charge not only of the great lines of domestic policy – the repression of the terrorists and the building of support among the peasantry – but also of the grinding minutiae of an overcentralized imperial bureaucracy. Everything came across his desk, from the issuing of passports to the regulation of veterinary surgeons. He was incapable of delegation and an omnivorous devourer of dossiers. Followed by a posse of note-taking assistants, he made the rounds of the assembly room outside his office every morning at eleven, listening personally to requests for pensions, concessions, clemency and jobs, dispensing rewards and punishments like an Asiatic grandee. The crazed and the discontented found their way to his office too, and in November, he had to duck when an assassin took aim at him. The bullet missed and killed his assistant instead.

Young Paul saw next to nothing of his father in that frantic year at the Ministry of the Interior. They lived in the family house at the junction of the Moika and Fontanka canals in a Petersburg gripped by rumours and plots and policed by soldiers at every corner. Paul was eleven that winter, just beginning his lessons at the gymnasium. One cold November afternoon, he was returning home from school in a little horse-drawn sleigh when he noticed that the Troitski Bridge, usually thronged with the carriages of the gentry and workers streaming home on foot, was strangely deserted. The police waved him onto the empty bridge and he began to cross. Halfway across, a magnificent carriage overtook him, and he just had time to spring to his feet and snap to attention as the imperial couple rolled past. The Tsarina smiled broadly at the little boy's frozen salute, but the Tsar was not amused. At his next meeting with his Minister of the Interior, he was not entirely mollified when told that the boy on the bridge had been the minister's son.

By the winter of 1882, Paul's father was at the pinnacle of his influence, the master of a vast apparatus of governors, spies, police agents and informers, the Tsar's chief source of information on the fevered state of his dominions. The immediate crisis of the autocracy seemed over. There were still some peasant pogroms against Jewish merchants in the southern provinces, but since these posed no direct threat to the regime itself, and since the peasants' grievances at Jewish millers, traders, bankers and merchants in the towns found sympathy in anti-Semitic ruling circles, the local police were less than assiduous in putting a stop to them.

Throughout the southern Ukraine and Bessarabia, Jewish shops were smashed and burned and crowds carrying icons, sometimes with priests at their head, were allowed to rampage through the Jewish quarters of the towns beating and cursing, looting and burning. Delegations of Jewish leaders came to see Ignatieff at the Ministry of the Interior. They told him they were in bondage as under Pharaoh. 'So when is your Exodus, and where is your Moses,' he is supposed to have asked them in reply. The western borders of the empire were open, he insisted. If they wanted to leave for their promised land, he would not stop them. And they did, by the hundreds of thousands over the next decade, streaming across Europe to the boats which took them to Ellis Island or to Palestine.

When the Jews asked why they were not entitled to the same protection by the police as other Russian subjects, Ignatieff replied that they were not like other Russian subjects. In May 1882, he signed new legislation forbidding Jews to move into the countryside outside the Pale of Jewish Settlement, to acquire land, to trade in alcohol, or to open their shops on Sundays. When Jewish leaders came to him and protested, pointing out that the measures reversed the slow, incremental liberalization of restrictions on Jews introduced by Tsar Alexander II during the 1860s, Ignatieff insisted that he had taken the new measures to 'protect' the Jews from peasant pogroms in the countryside. To the Tsar himself, Ignatieff justified the decrees with memos that

painted a familiar fantasy of a Jewish–Polish conspiracy with its
hands on 'the banks, the stock exchange, the bar, and a great part
of the press', a conspiracy that plundered the state treasury and
preached 'blind imitation of Europe'. The new legislation would
remove 'the abnormal conditions which exist between Jews and
natives and protect the latter from the pernicious activity . . .
which was responsible for the disturbances'.

This was the dark side of Ignatieff's pan-Slavism, the un-
acceptable face of the Orthodox nationalism that had made him
an empire builder in Asia and a supporter of the Slavic Christian
cause against the Turks. He gave respectability to the prejudices
of his time and class, hoping that he could build himself an
unassailable position with the Tsar in a Petersburg milieu seeth-
ing with intrigues against him. But by May 1882 it became more
and more difficult to keep his balance in the infighting of the
court. Konstantin Pobedonostsev, the Tsar's former tutor and
chief confidant, once Ignatieff's champion, became jealous of his
influence and began to plot his downfall, scheming openly with
the prefect of the Petersburg police. The Tsar himself, large,
cautious and stupid, became resentful of the elegant verbal turns
of a minister who seemed to think of himself as the autocracy's
saviour.

Sensing that his time might be running out, Ignatieff chanced
everything on a final throw of the dice. He drafted a statute for the
convocation of a *zemski sobor*, an assembly which would bring
together representatives from the peasantry, the merchant guilds
and the landed proprietors to listen obediently to the Tsar's plans
for his empire, to offer respectful advice and to join with him in
healing the rift between the autocracy and society. It was not to be
a parliament with legislative or deliberative powers. Ignatieff
shared the Slavophile suspicion of European democracy, with
its unseemly popular clamours and open political discussion.
Instead, the convocation of the *zemski sobor* was conceived of as
a romantic gesture of political reconciliation, an attempt to meet
the universal demand for political renewal by bringing back the

good old days when Muscovite tsars met their boyars in a *zemski sobor* upon their coronation.

Ignatieff begged the Tsar to keep his plans secret from Pobedonostsev and the court clique plotting against him. But when he came to the Cabinet room to discuss his proposals one May morning in 1882, he found a draft of the document open before every place and understood from the triumphant looks of Pobedonostsev and his clique that the game was up. When the Tsar asked him to begin discussion of the document, Ignatieff rose and left the room. He was never to return. At exactly fifty years of age, on the eve of an action that he believed would save the autocracy, he was dismissed by the Tsar and sent packing to his estates.

For a man whose blood needed the oxygen of power, banishment was like a stroke. It aged him overnight. For a decade more, he schemed and struggled to return to the centre of power. He sat in his study with his Khivan swords, his Chinese silks and the portrait of William Ewart Gladstone and wrote up his memoirs of his Asian adventures and long defences of his achievements in Constantinople. He gave interviews to foreign journalists and used their columns shamelessly to promote his own return to power. The Slavonic Society made him president of their association and they provided him with a platform for orotund addresses. Afterwards they always carried him shoulder high to his carriage. But he was not fooled. By 1890, he knew he was finished.

In his feverish way, he turned some of his vagrant energies loose upon his children. He was a disciplinarian in the home and banned cards, liquor, swearing and cigarettes. His son Paul remembered the night in his teens when two grand dukes came to a dance at the family house and set out after dinner to test his father's insistence that no pack of cards was to be found in the place. The dukes set off down the dark servants' passage, rummaging through closets, opening doors, peeking into darkened rooms. Monsieur Castellot went into a boxer's crouch when they burst into his bedroom and they backed away down the passage. Eventually they found a greasy old deck in a janitor's office across the courtyard and returned triumphantly to the drawing room, one of them holding it between thumb and finger.

Paul's father enforced a spartan regime on his children: Bible lessons with his mother, lean food, cold baths, riding, fencing, and cold winter walks in the streets of Petersburg to build up the legs and the lungs. Paul became so cold on one of these enforced winter outings that Monsieur Castellot had to pick him up, bundle him inside his coat and carry him all the way home.

Paul was an anxious, sickly child, given to asthma attacks, gastric pains and the occasional dead faint. He had learned to sail during summers on the Bosphorus and in the Crimea and had wanted to take up a career in the navy, but his father gruffly ruled out a sea career on the grounds that his constitution would not stand it.

Seen in the glare of Freudian retrospect, Paul's adolescent symptoms – the shortness of breath, the fainting – seem to be his body's protest at his father's suffocating presence. For the father was an awesome figure and the stories he now told in peevish middle age were of just the kind to reduce a loving son to suffocated silence: how he had ridden across Asia in six weeks, how he had bested Bismarck, dined with Disraeli. Hemmed in on the one side by older brothers who were beginning their careers in the Guards, and on the other by this father whose relentless energy seemed to mock his own quieter, more reflective disposition, Paul grew into his teens an anxious, earnest boy, happiest in the estate in the Ukraine, away from the pressures of his lessons, society dances and his father.

Paul's mother was a warmer presence, but she too was a formidable figure. Her children were never allowed to forget that she was Marshal Kutuzov's great-granddaughter. Characteristically, Paul's strongest memory of her from childhood was of her on a horse. During the summers at Kroupodernitsa, whenever she announced that she wished to go riding, Paul would race down to the stables to help the grooms saddle up her favourite bay, Djirid. He helped the grooms saddle-train the horse, riding side-saddle with rags tied to his belt to accustom the animal to the rustle of her riding costume against its flanks. He always remembered how she strode up to the horse in her riding costume, whip in hand, placed her boot in the cupped hands of the coachman and gracefully vaulted up into the saddle. In his earliest memory, she is seated daintily on her side-saddle, whip in hand, looking down at him with tender amusement.

During his first term at the law faculty in Petersburg Paul came down with an asthma attack which forced him to withdraw. It occurred again when he enrolled in the second year. It was as if his breath failed him scaling the heights set out for him by his father. In November 1889, the family despatched him to Paris, to the clinic of Europe's leading specialist in nervous diseases, Jean-Martin Charcot. 'La chose génitale, toujours, toujours!', Sigmund Freud remembered Charcot muttering during a consultation on the causes of hysteria in women at the Salpêtrière Hospital. There were male hysterics as well, and it is possible that some part of Paul's symptoms was hysterical. In any event, for six months Paul, then nineteen, lived in Charcot's rest home in Passy. For company he had his old tutor Monsieur Castellot, himself recovering from a buckshot wound in his backside incurred while out on one of his hunting expeditions. They went to the theatre at night and by day followed the regime of plain food, bed rest and quiet walks designed to calm the nervous system. But when Paul took his leave in the spring of 1890, Charcot examined him and confessed that he had only managed a partial cure. 'Spasmodic symptoms', he warned, were bound to recur. Stay away from Petersburg and all city excitements, he ordered. Bury yourself in the country.

Paul did exactly that. He rented one of his father's dilapidated estates near Kroupodernitsa and after purchasing some worn-out nags and second-hand machinery, he hired some local peasants to plant him his first crop. The beasts rolled over and went to sleep at the end of the furrows and had to be beaten to their feet, and the first crop that spring was miserable, but he persevered and by the end of the next year, he could reasonably claim to have made himself into a gentleman farmer. He lived like this for several years, wintering in Petersburg to complete his law studies, and then spending spring and summer at the estate, often working side by side with his hired hands in the fields.

He had discovered Tolstoy during those winter months in the rest home in Passy. When the Tolstoyan impulse of getting back to the people was fused with the pan-Slavist nostalgia for the peasantry he had inherited from his father, the result was a new set of convictions that were to remain with him all his life. Russian society was sick with the divide between aristocrat and peasant, and the Russian aristocrat himself was sick from his fatal divorce from the soil. Paul's father at first approved these sentiments but eventually became alarmed at how far his son seemed prepared to take them. Actually guiding a plough through the furrows side by side with his peasant employees seemed to be carrying conviction too far.

Paul's closest friend from the law faculty in Petersburg, Vladimir Nabokov, also thought his friend's passion for farming was baffling. A man should be interested in tennis, in literature, in politics, not in manure and seeds. When Nabokov visited Kroupodernitsa in the summer holidays, he would sit under an umbrella in the cabriolet in a broad-brimmed hat and a cream linen suit and read while his earnest friend in the heavy corduroys discussed seed-drilling techniques with his peasant foremen in the dusty beet fields.

In the railway carriage carrying them back to their studies in Petersburg, the two friends argued about literature and politics. Paul particularly remembered a conversation which lasted through the night about Tolstoy's short story 'The Kreutzer Sonata', a polemic against the sexual enslavement of marriage. Paul remembered insisting that he would model his life on Tolstoy's teaching, and when he got back to Petersburg, he did just that. He announced, somewhat sententiously, that he would remain a bachelor and when a coy female cousin asked him to write an inscription in her commonplace book he wrote a furious Tolstoyan epigram that was to guide him grimly through life:

Life is not a game, life is not a joke.
Renunciation! Renunciation!
It is only by putting on the chains of service that man can fulfil his destiny on earth.

This was the earnest, ascetic young man who reported for military service at the Gatchina headquarters of the Preobrajensky Guards in the summer of 1894. He loved his military service, the singsongs with his recruits, the hard physical drill, the rhythmic tramping of the boots on the parade ground, the sweat running down between his shoulderblades; and at the end of a long day, a cup of coffee in a tent he had hung with Ukrainian rugs. It was at the end of such a day, with the coffeepot brewing on the stove, that the tent flaps parted and the young lieutenant found himself staring at his commandant and the heir to the throne, the future Nicholas II. They asked if they could have a cup of coffee. While Paul was busying himself with the coffee, the commandant asked him to explain to the heir to the throne why the autocracy was so unpopular in Russia. Paul handed his guests their cups of coffee and said quietly, 'If you mean the personal autocracy of the sovereign, you are probably wrong. The majority of Russians understand that the head of such a vast country with a mixed population must have the necessary power. What they do resent is the autocracy of the scribe, the policeman, the governor and even the minister.' The commandant laughed and the heir to the throne gave Paul one of his thin and impassive blue stares. Neither Paul nor, as it turned out, the heir to the throne forgot what had passed between them.

Paul's military service was soon over and he returned to Kroupodernitsa to the life of a bachelor farmer and a dutiful son. His brothers had married and had begun their careers in the army and the navy. Sister Katia was training to be a nurse, and Paul and sister Mika were left at Kroupodernitsa to attend their parents' slow decline and listen to their father's muddled recriminations. By this time, the old man's business affairs were in a mess. His steward, Grinevetsky, was swindling him openly and Paul had to mortgage estates to keep the creditors at bay. Old age and twenty years' exile from power had broken his father's morale.

There is a picture taken at the turn of the century of Paul's parents standing together in one of the chestnut alleys of the garden at Kroupodernitsa. The serene beauty whom the fine ladies of Hatfield House strove to emulate thirty years before is stout now, her hair grey and covered with a white shawl. Her husband leans heavily on her arm. He wears a plain white field cap, an unbraided army greatcoat and carpet slippers. His eyes are rheumy and resentful, glaring ahead at the dreary and foregone battle of aging. He who had once been so adventurous, so daring, wearing out post horses in every sordid inn from Irkutsk to Petersburg, is now at last unrelievedly old.

By then his kidneys and bladder were beginning to give out. In the winter of 1903 he went to Paris for an operation, and commanded Paul to join him on the Riviera to keep him company during his convalescence and to massage his gouty feet. When Paul was boarding the European express headed for Vienna and Cannes that January of 1903, one of the old Tartar waiters in the station restaurant, who had served the family since Paul was a boy, called out that Paul should get himself married. 'Only fools marry!' Paul shouted back as the train pulled out.

FOUR
PAUL AND NATASHA

⸺

In January 1903, Natasha and her mother set out from her Moscow home to catch the train for the Riviera. After a chaotic procession of family and servants to the station in the snow, embraces and blessings on the platform, and after settling her mother in her compartment, Natasha sat back in peace, enfolded in the sealed world of the sleeping car, with its brown plush seats, washbasins and divans. For the empty hours until nightfall she watched the snow-bound Russian plain fly past her window. At dawn at the German border, she lay in her bed and felt the train being transferred from its broad Russian gauge to the narrower European one. It was like going to sleep in one century and waking up in another when the maternal rocking of the Russian gauges was replaced by the sharper gyration of the European lines. She changed trains in Paris and drifted asleep in the dark panelled compartments of the sleeping car while it awaited the departure whistle in the Gare de Lyon. At first light she lifted the blind at the end of the bed with her toe and as the train sped round the cliffs and through the tunnels, she saw the waves of the Mediterranean so close they seemed to be beating at her window.

Her Riviera smelled of the grey dust thrown up behind the carriages, the petals cascading upon her during the *bataille des fleurs* at Mardi Gras and incense at the Orthodox cathedral in Nice. In those days, Cannes and Nice were quiet, restful places, the long afternoons before tea punctuated by the sound of horses' hooves and the creaking of the fiacres carrying families from one big hotel to another. For Natasha and her mother the Riviera season began in January and ended in April: they came for the sea air and the weak winter sunlight on the promenades, for the gossip and companionship of the Russian restaurants, churches and bookshops, and above all, to escape the darkness and cold of Moscow and Petersburg. That winter of 1903, they came because Princess Mestchersky, Natasha's mother, knew that this visit would be her last. The respite from cancer which the operations had brought her was now coming to an end.

Natasha's mother had always admired the stout nationalist sentiments of General Nicholas Ignatieff. She had once presented him with a bouquet of flowers after an address he had given to the Slavonic Society in Moscow. So when General Ignatieff and his wife, who happened to be wintering at the Grand Hôtel de Californie in Cannes, sent a servant to the Mestchersky villa in Nice requesting that they visit them, Natasha's mother said she was too weak to go, but Natasha would be delighted to accept. Natasha was not so delighted, but there was no arguing with mother. She could not go alone and so her brother Peter chaperoned her on the hour-long carriage ride along the coast road from Nice to Cannes.

Natasha was exchanging tense pleasantries with General Ignatieff and his wife in the palm court of the Hôtel de Californie when a slim tall man in his early thirties, with a moustache and a sailor's tan on his high balding forehead, descended the main staircase and came towards her. When he smiled his teeth were very white, his eyes dark.

At that meeting, Paul and Natasha were shy and formal, sitting apart, exchanging glances while her brother Peter carried on with the exchange of ritual pleasantries with the Ignatieffs. When they rose to leave, Paul bowed, kissed her hand and said he hoped he would have the pleasure again. She blushed and bowed her head. All the way home, Peter teased his old spinster of a sister for that blush and she was furious with herself for having given herself away.

Next day, Paul appeared at the door of the Mestchersky villa in Nice and sent up his card. She received him in a little sitting room and shyly served him tea. He returned next day and the day after. In matters of courtship, they were a backward couple. He was earnest and serious, she was shy. Other Russians gamed at the tables in Monte Carlo, or dressed up in costumes and joined the carnival crowds. Paul and Natasha stayed away from the dances and the gaming tables. They walked together on the balcony of the casino at night overlooking the bay. They were moving closer but not yet touching, silently watching the lights of the yachts at anchor, listening to the whir of the gaming wheels.

When they first met, the Mestcherskys whispered that the Ignatieffs were ruined. With muddled indirection Natasha raised the question of Ignatieff family finance. Like a good Edwardian suitor, Paul assured her of his prospects. It is doubtful that he told her everything and it did not occur to him to ask himself whether this princess raised on a huge estate would be able to manage on a working farm in the depths of the Ukraine.

Paul and Natasha were soon aware that those two old nineteenth-century warships – the Ignatieff and Mestchersky families – were being surreptitiously manoeuvred alongside each other. Natasha began to feel the new undertow in her mother's talk: the hints, the looks, the sighs of a dying woman eager to see her youngest settled in time. Paul's father, for his part, was so worried that his son's Tolstoyan vows of celibacy might still carry the day that he wired Paul's old tutor Monsieur Castellot to come down from Paris and talk some sense into his son. Monsieur Castellot did not have to do much persuading.

On 19 February, two weeks after their meeting, Paul and Natasha went for a walk together in Chaplitz park above Nice, with her brother Peter and his brother Vladimir – on leave from the Russian fleet docked in the Riviera – bringing up the rear as chaperons. Paul sat her down on a bench beneath a lemon tree and began what she thought was to be a proposal of marriage. First he became entangled in a long and far-fetched story about motorcars and then he managed to leave Natasha thinking that she wasn't to be his life's companion after all. All that the chaperons could see was that Natasha had risen stiffly to her feet and that Paul sat stricken on the bench. Paul's brother Vladimir, sensing the turn events had taken, stepped up brightly and accompanied Natasha home, filling her silent distress with welcome chatter about his Pekinese dog. Recalling the scene at the end of her life, she added mournfully, 'Maybe for Paul's future happiness it would be better if everything had been broken between us.' At her doorway, she whispered to Vladimir that she would be pleased to go for a walk again the following day.

Next morning at nine Vladimir and Paul appeared at the door, mackintoshes draped over their arms. It had rained, but the morning was bright and pungent. She was ready, so was her brother Peter, and they set off up the old road to Cimiez. This time they did not have to travel far. He put the question clearly. She answered clearly. Her brother, Peter, who had been bringing up the rear, sighed with relief when he saw them at last holding hands and smiling shyly. 'At least my last pair of boots has been saved in time.' For his engagement present, he gave them a miniature replica in silver of the shoes he had worn out trudging behind them as chaperon.

For the next three weeks until their wedding, Paul would appear at nine at the Mestchersky villa in Nice with lilies he had chosen in the flower market of the old port. They would sit together in the front room, learning to relax in each other's company. They could now laugh at the gossip each family had heard about the other. He brought her a little brooch shaped like a cornflower because, he said, the cornflowers which grew among his wheat back home were his favourite flower. Natasha ordered her trousseau linen from Dresden, where the family crest was embroidered on the sheets and pillowcases, and her personal linen from Rouff in Nice. She ordered a travelling trunk from a shop in the rue St Honoré in Paris.

These weeks just before their marriage were to be the only extended time they had alone together for the next twenty years. 'My husband never belonged to himself,' she said with some little irony, 'always serving the state and his countrymen.' Duty, duty. He did not belong to himself. He did not belong to her.

In the gamble of marriage, theirs was a blind throw. Their courtship and engagement lasted barely a month. What could she have seen beneath his earnest smiling surface? He was as contained as his father was expansive. They were drawn to each other by what had been repressed in each, he to that mordant gaiety which lay concealed beneath her shy exterior, she to his practicality and charm which seemed to hint of physical gentleness to come.

They were married at a little Orthodox church on the rue Longchamps in Nice on 16 April 1903. She wore a white crepe-de-Chine dress with a long train. She carried a small wreath of orange blossoms and there were more orange blossoms in her hair. Her face was wreathed in a veil which Paul pulled back when he kissed her at the altar. She felt calm and disembodied, numb as a piece of wood. Her feelings, she said, always seemed to desert her at the most important moments of her life. Of the whole climactic day, she remembered only that she was very hungry and gobbled up pâté sandwiches at the reception afterwards. Later that afternoon, a landau laden with cornflowers took them along the coast road from Cannes to the Hôtel Cap d'Antibes for their honeymoon.

After a week walking together by the sea, they returned to the Ukraine. At the station, the old Tartar waiter who had seen Paul off to the Riviera two months before called from the restaurant window when Paul passed by with his bride: 'Remember, only fools marry!' As she walked along the platform towards the Ignatieffs, their voices already booming out their greetings, she felt her face become a mask and her timid soul hide away. She had dreaded this plunge into a huge and alien family, thousands of miles from Doughino. Paul's brothers and sisters, his mother and father were there and their kisses, embraces and covert hard looks were, she said later, the 'expiation of all her sins'.

At each thatched, whitewashed cottage on the road to the

estate, Paul lifted the young bride down from the carriage and presented her to the peasant couple standing in the doorway. From each they received the traditional round loaf of bread, with a salt cellar cut deep into the loaf, presented on an embroidered tablecloth, then they kissed the icons of the house laid out on a table by the doorway. As godfather to the village children, master of the village choir and largest employer in the district, Paul knew each man and woman by their names and father's names. At dusk while she sat with her new family on the veranda, the village choir serenaded them with Ukrainian songs. They went to bed with the cheers the choir had raised to their choirmaster's happiness ringing in their ears.

Next morning when she awoke in the small bright bedroom, she was alone. Paul was already downstairs on the porch receiving the first of the peasant delegations, listening to complaints, accepting petitions, meeting with the estate managers about the stock and the spring planting. He had been away for months. Everything had to be taken in hand again. When she came down to breakfast, she was seized with fear that she had lost him, that the week just passed in the Hôtel Cap d'Antibes had now slipped beyond reach.

Everything in the Ukraine was strange to her: the jabber of Ukrainian dialects from the peasants and servants; the heavily accented Russian of their Polish landowner neighbours; the talk of seed drills and tractors and stockbreeding around the table; even the strange wood carvings on the roof of the big house. On Sundays in the family church, the family would file past the priest, kissing the cross, General Ignatieff and his wife first, then their sons and daughters, then the peasants after them. And as they left church, the villagers would kiss the Ignatieffs' hands at the church door: in Doughino, the peasants did not kiss hands. She felt she had returned to the Middle Ages.

Perhaps the family thought her snobbish, standoffish, this princess from the great estate near Smolensk. Certainly Kroupodernitsa was smaller than Doughino: a solid, three-storey country house, comfortable but not luxurious or ancient. She admitted it was 'cosy', but she could never feel at home there. At one end of the dinner table sat her mother-in-law, her grey hair always covered by a white shawl; at the other, slumped and brooding, sat her father-in-law, the old general. She felt pity for him. The whispering and the ridicule which followed each of his catastrophic financial adventures left Paul's father peevish and embittered. Yet there was still fire in him, and after dinner, with the family spread out around him on the veranda, he could still conjure up his great days in central Asia, in Peking and in the Turkish war. Even in his ruin Natasha felt he was the most forceful personality – with the exception of her own mother – she was ever to meet in her life.

Paul took his young bride driving along the dusty roads at dusk in the family brougham, past the oak woods at Bossibrod, to the little towns round about, Ouman, Lipovetz. On the warm afternoons of early summer, he rowed her along the marshy banks of the river and showed her where he used to hunt with Monsieur Castellot. He showed her the stables where he had once broken in his father's new Arab stallions and he tried in vain to interest her in riding. His boyhood was all around him. But her childhood was far away in the manicured lawns and greenhouses of Doughino. As much as she wanted to, she couldn't share his passion for the Ukraine. She missed Doughino, she pined for her mother. In those first months at Kroupodernitsa, her eyes were often red from crying. Once, sitting alone in the study dabbing her cheeks with a handkerchief, Natasha heard a knock at the door and before she could compose herself found herself face to face with Paul's mother. Countess Ignatieff gave her a cool, appraising stare. Natasha looked back at her in mute supplication.

The doors back to Natasha's past began ciosing behind her just as the new life stretching before her seemed to become ever more strained. In September 1903 Natasha raced back to Doughino to be at her mother's bedside in her final hours. She was already expecting her first child and she thought of her child as a gift to lay in her mother's arms. But the gift arrived too late. Her mother was able to order her grandson's trousseau but cancer had taken possession of her and she died that month with Natasha and her sisters at her side. When Natasha drove out between the great white gates of Doughino the day after the funeral, she took away with her a photograph album of the park, the greenhouses and the luminous and vacant rooms shining with imperishable light. She never returned.

In that miserable autumn of 1903, once more in the Ukraine, grieving for her mother, nauseous from morning sickness, she helped her sisters-in-law to run a day school for peasant children in harvesting time. She hated chasing after the little wretches in her stiff new clothes through the prickly stubble by the river's edge. She pined for someone to confide in but Paul was always riding off to Ouman or Lipovetz, to oversee the recruiting of peasants, to collect taxes and tithes or to adjudicate some boundary dispute involving the peasants. Countess Ignatieff, with experience of six children behind her, could have allayed Natasha's fears of a first pregnancy but she kept her own icy counsel.

Natasha turned to Mika, Paul's sister, for companionship, but she lived behind a screen of duty, bustling off every morning in her pony and trap with medicines and bandages to tend the children in the village and to inspect the hospitals and schools the family had built around the estate. Mika worshipped her brother Paul, and Natasha could sense that she had been judged and found wanting. Yet gradually as Natasha's pregnancy progressed, Mika began to thaw. She brought Natasha a plant from a barefoot pilgrim at the church door who said it had been picked in Jerusalem. It would flower, the pilgrim had told her, and its flowering would ensure Natasha a painless delivery. Through the autumn of 1903, she waited. The flower did not open.

Paul's older sister Katia was an even more commanding and austere figure than Mika. She was a trained nurse who had tended typhus victims among the foreign troops in Manchuria during the Boxer Rebellion in 1898. In the photo albums of those early years at Kroupodernitsa, Katia – or Countess Kitty as the servants called her – stares out at the camera with a forceful look, the keys of the house dangling on a chain down the front of a severe black dress, her face tight with determination and her eyes ringed with sadness.

She looked very different in a picture taken about ten years earlier in the 1890s at a fancy-dress ball at the home of the Grand Duke Michael in Petersburg. She was nineteen then, a gentle oval-faced beauty, with thin wispy hair pulled back off her face and round wounded eyes. In the photograph, she is reclining at the Grand Duke's feet in a brocade ball gown, while he leans on a trestle table crowded with other guests, all in Renaissance costume. The Grand Duke had been in love with her then, and she with him, and in the photograph she seems to stare longingly at a future that she could not allow herself to believe in. It was not to be. The Grand Duke was a member of the royal family and the Tsar apparently forbade the match. Michael went to live abroad and Katia went round the world to try to forget. When she returned, she had renounced her gentle wounded self and became instead practical, level-headed Countess Kitty. Yet in the eyes that stare out of the later photographs, just a trace of the impossible wishes of a nineteen-year-old still remained. She threw herself into a round of duty at the estate and in January 1904, when the Japanese forces attacked the Russian naval base at Port Arthur and began the Russo-Japanese War, she rushed by train to Vladivostok to enlist as a nurse.

It was within a month of Port Arthur – as the country strained and snapped in the gale that was to end with the revolution of 1905 – that Natasha gave birth to her first son. She knew nothing about childbearing and wanted to know as little as possible. Like harbingers of doom, the forceps, bandages and scalpels arrived at Kroupodernitsa by coach from Kiev followed next day by a jewelled society midwife who announced that Natasha should be quick about it because she was loath to spend a second longer in the godforsaken Ukraine than necessary. Through one long night of labour, Paul read verses from the Bible to comfort Natasha, while an evil-smelling local doctor stood by and the decrepit society midwife held Natasha in her arms and shook with terror at her screams.

The baby boy, Nicholas, was safely delivered, but Natasha was left damaged by the birth and her beauty, as she put it, 'quite packed up'. All spring and summer, she sat on the veranda convalescing, watching the peasant women coming up from their cottages to water the garden at nightfall. They bent low over the pool in the garden to scoop up buckets of water and carry them to the long rows of sweet peas, tuberoses and madonna lilies. She sat by the cot in her white crinolines in the veranda's shade and wondered if birth was the same for peasant women as it had been for her. These women bending over the pool in her garden seemed so strong. It came as a shock when a local doctor told her that most of them were broken at forty from childbearing and overwork.

Natasha felt no wave of maternal feeling at first, just a kind of pity at how pathetic her little son seemed, lying helplessly in his cot, sniffling and breathing like a puppy. She had not wanted a child so soon. She wanted to hold on to her life alone with Paul a little longer, to prolong the spell of their courtship. But it was not to be. In the first thirteen years of marriage, she was pregnant at least nine times. She hated and dreaded 'the whole business', and at the same time tormented herself with the thought that she was failing him. Their sexual life together was cursed by quack doctors, by the unhappy fate of easy fertility and by an unbreachable gulf between Paul's passionate and demanding sexuality and her retiring and aversive physical nature.

She was glad in the autumn of 1904 when Paul's new post as chairman of the *zemstvo* – the local government board – for the province required them to leave the Ignatieffs at Kroupodernitsa and live alone together in Kiev. At last she could be under her

[75]

own roof, away from the rule of her mother-in-law. The two years in the sunny little flat on Levashkovskaya street in the Lipki, the leafy residential quarter of the city built on the bluffs overlooking the Dnieper, were a happy dream for her. For once she felt she was a partner in his work: visiting the hospitals and institutions administered by the *zemstvo*, and entertaining the *zemstvo* workers at the end of the day with *piroshki* and beer.

Paul threw himself into the work. He dashed out early in the morning with his sandwiches and newspaper, walking the short distance to the *zemstvo* offices in the City Hall Square, returning at night to work on papers in his study. There were hospitals to build; only one general hospital existed to serve the four and a half million people of Kiev province; the country roads had to be surveyed and resurfaced; sugar-beet cooperatives were opened; rural fire insurance was reorganized to give the peasants protection for their thatched cottages; the forced-labour system used to maintain the roads, provide horses for the post chaise, even to transport criminals, was replaced by a rural tax system. It was work of detail, the practical business of bringing his country into the twentieth century, and Paul loved every minute of it. He prided himself on being a practical farmer, a man from the provinces, who knew how to run combine harvesters, when to plant beets, how to talk to peasants in the field, how to get the best out of a man. He discovered his own capacities for leadership, assembling round him a core of vets, agronomists, surveyors, teachers and doctors who were devoted to 'the liberalism of small deeds'. These were the *zemstvo* professionals – resented by the Petersburg bureaucracy, scorned by the revolutionaries in Zürich and Bern – who were trying to lead their old country along the path of quiet, unspectacular rural modernization. They prayed for time: every new cooperative, factory, hospital needed a decade for its harvest.

All of this steady work occurred against the increasingly sombre backdrop of the Russo-Japanese War. The *zemstvos* had been asked to take care of all the dependents of the soldiers sent from the province to the battlefields of Manchuria, but without any resources to help them complete the task. Paul travelled to Petersburg with other *zemstvo* leaders to demand assistance from the central government. When an official from the Department of Finance protested that the *zemstvos* were failing in their patriotic duty, and added, 'This is not the spirit that prevails in Japan!' Paul shot back across the table, 'We know of only one measure taken to strengthen the finance of the country to enable it to carry on the war, the tax on matches!'

From Katia's letters written from Vladivostok, Paul could sense how badly the war was going. There was a shortage of everything: weapons, bandages, field glasses, cannon, boots. Most of the commanders had not seen service since the Russo-Turkish War and were stunned by the new kind of war the Japanese were waging. Yet the staff officers' talk in the mess was full of blithe assumptions of Slavic racial superiority over the yellow enemy and the patriotic press was full of perverse confidence in the virtues of Russian backwardness, in the peasant bayonet charge against the machine gun. At home in Kiev, Paul heard the peasant recruits being loaded on to the trains wondering why they were having to die in the east. It was rumoured that the country had been lured into conflict by the Tsar's desire to protect a consortium of concession hunters who were seeking control of forest rights in Korea, which traditionally had been under the Japanese sphere of influence. This consortium included Paul's own uncle, the rotund and reactionary General Alexis Ignatieff, former governor general of Western Siberia, now a member of the State Council.

Paul's brother Vladimir joined the Russian fleet which set sail from the Baltic to travel around the world to engage the Japanese in the waters off China. In letters mailed from the coastal coaling stations, which found their way to the fastness of the Ukraine, the family followed the fleet's progress down the African coast, around the Horn, across the Indian Ocean to its fateful meeting with the Japanese. For Vladimir's mother each letter was a torment: Vladimir was her youngest, the one who had always known how to reach her armoured heart. Each letter became gloomier as the fatal engagement approached: the ships were old, they manoeuvred poorly, the crews were exhausted.

At the dockside in Vladivostok, one July day in 1905, Katia and the nurses from the marine hospital were told to await the Russian fleet's arrival. All day Katia scanned the grey horizon for ships' funnels, for the wisps of smoke which would herald her brother's safe passage through the fire. At dusk she knew there would be no ships. The horizon was empty. The Japanese had destroyed the Russian fleet in the battle of Tsushima. Vladimir, chief officer on the admiral's flagship, went down with his ship. His last letters, full of the strained cheerfulness of a child keeping his courage up, arrived at Kroupodernitsa after the news of his death. Outside the church in Kroupodernitsa, the family raised a monument to him, a cross on a plinth of basalt, with a ship's anchor at the base. It is still there, at the edge of wheat fields, 500 miles from the sea. At the end of August, Paul and Natasha's second child was born in Kiev, and they named him Vladimir. At his christening Paul placed the infant in his mother's arms and said to her, 'Here is your new Vladimir.'

A month later, in early September 1905, Natasha was back in Kiev in the apartment on Levashkovskaya street, with little Vladimir in her arms and Nicholas, then a year and a half old, at her feet, when she saw from the upstairs window a strange procession slowly approaching up the street. They were poor people mostly, marching in rows, singing hymns, carrying icons and 'hideous cheap reproductions of the Tsar'. She sent her valet down to see what was happening. Someone in the crowd told him to get inside. Then the rocks began to fly through the air and the glass in the house opposite belonging to a Jewish merchant started breaking. It seemed fantastic and surreal, this sudden irruption of riot into the little frame of Natasha's existence. As the glass crashed in the street below her and looters began climbing in through the shattered windows, the crowd sang hymns

Natasha had known from childhood. Nicholas stood with his nose to the window and shouted 'Hurrah!' In a corner of the nursery away from the windows sat the boys' old nurse, rocking to and fro, her lips soundlessly whispering a prayer.

Someone went down and remonstrated with the crowd, saying it was unchristian to destroy people's property. Natasha held her children tight, watching the scene. She was safe, perched just above the storm. Someone in the crowd daubed a white cross on the gate of their house. They would be spared. Slowly and methodically, the procession moved down the street to the next Jewish house. While some smashed the windows with stones and others leaped in to begin looting, the rest stood outside and sang hymns. The police did not arrive until it was all over. After the last of the procession had gone, Natasha's valet told her that the Jewish woman who lived opposite had come to the door and begged that they shelter her children from the crowd. The woman could hear the procession coming up the street. She was desperate. The valet refused to let them in without Count Ignatieff's orders and he was at work. She appealed to Natasha's landlady. 'My babies have scarlet fever, hide them,' she pleaded. In that case, the landlady said, she could not admit children suffering from scarlet fever. There were other children in the house to think of. The mother and her children managed to flee into town as the crowd began pitching stones at her house.

Paul returned home breathless late that night. A crowd had burst into his office at the *zemstvo*, pulled out the telephones and demanded that all the *zemstvo* workers join the general strike. Paul refused to negotiate with a crowd, but offered to talk to three of their leaders. A peasant member of the *zemstvo* board began arguing with one of the student leaders of the crowd. 'You are Jewish, you have no right to represent Russians,' the peasant shouted. The meeting was in uproar. Then shouts were heard from the crowd: bearing down on them in the street were five Cossacks, standing up in their stirrups, whips poised to strike.

[79]

Paul opened a back door and let the crowd's leaders vanish down a side street.

The city was ablaze with anti-Semitic rumour. A Jewish lawyer named Ratner was supposed to have raced down the main street of the city, the Krestchatik, on a white charger, shouting, 'We gave you the Saviour; now we will give you a new Tsar.' That night Paul and Natasha's maid served dinner wearing a new wristwatch. She had picked it up from among the shattered glass and gashed awnings of the Jewish jewellers on the Krestchatik. In the countryside, revolutionary bandits were burning cooperatives and factories and holding up banks. Peasants were seizing the lands of absentee landlords. A peasant delegation came to meet the *zemstvo* board, and Paul always remembered how one of them told a grim little parable. 'When food is abundant in the summer, the worker bees are satisfied to feed the queen bee and the drones, but when autumn comes and food gets scarce, what happens to the drones?' In the silence, the peasant snapped his fingers ominously and said, 'Out they go.'

Natasha watched the revolution of 1905 unfolding with angry disbelief. 'Things were just left unchecked at the beginning,' she wrote later. 'From the throne on down, there was always the same total lack of strength, power and organization: things just floating away at their own, drifting away hopelessly.'

In January 1906, Paul's uncle Alexis was named governor of Tver province. He had a reputation for reaction and for severity with political prisoners dating back to his days as governor of Western Siberia. Soon after his arrival to take up his post in Tver, he walked into a university reception and was stopped by a student who approached for a few words. The student pulled out a revolver and shot Alexis dead at point-blank range. When arrested the student was found to have connections both with the Socialist Revolutionaries and with the secret police.

It was at this moment – in a city torn by riot and pogrom, in a country lurching on the edge of a precipice – that Paul was appointed governor of the province of Kiev, a territory the size of

Great Britain. At first, Natasha was loath to leave the little flat on Levashkovskaya for the governor's mansion, with its formal and cheerless rooms filled with busts of the Tsar. And at first, the times were frightening: plots, rumours of plots, coaches following behind their own at night when they returned from the theatre, threatening letters arriving with the morning mail, obscene and vicious notes which she would drop on to the silver tray as if she had been scalded.

Later, they were happy in the governor's house, now ringing with the sound of three little boys, Nicholas, Vladimir and Alec, and a baby Paul. Downstairs, outside the governor's study, the courier Abraham, who looked like an old black crow, would screen the petitioners lining up outside the door, while Natasha worked in a study of her own with her friend Madame Zabougina organizing charity bazaars and fêtes on behalf of the local hospitals and orphanages. She felt happiest when Paul was in the house, when they seemed to be working side by side. At nights they would sometimes go to the opera house in Kiev, and she remembered that she once saw Sarah Bernhardt and once heard the great Russian singer Chaliapin. There were cruises on the Dnieper in the yachts of millionaires, nights under the stars in their fragrant garden; there was time for each other.

Paul had been chosen as a man with a local, liberal reputation to bring peace to the city, and so he did. An old monk who had been stirring up anti-Semitic hatred with his Sunday sermons was brought into his office and told to cease preaching that the Jews had crucified Jesus. The head of the local right-wing vigilantes, the Black Hundreds, was told that he would be held personally responsible if another Jewish shop was attacked. The police commander was told to patrol the Jewish section of the city in person and to instruct his men that they faced instant dismissal if they failed to put down attacks on Jewish homes and businesses.

When students at Kiev University occupied the buildings, Paul ordered his cavalry to surround the lecture halls to persuade them to come out peacefully and then march them all off to the

armoury for a hot meal and a bed. The non-student revolutionaries were identified and prosecuted; the students returned to
class. When a Polish landowner's son wounded a peasant girl on a
shooting expedition and her village responded by burning down
the landowner's house, Paul despatched a squadron of Cossacks
to arrest the landowner's son and to force the village to deliver up
the arsonists. When a revolutionary gang robbed a sugar-beet
factory, killing two night watchmen, his police pursued the men
to Odessa, arrested them and secured their conviction. They
escaped his death sentence by taking poison in the cells.

As civilian governor Paul had the power to ban any demonstrations and break up any meetings he considered a threat to the
public peace. He could even shut down the *zemstvo* he himself
had led and his police could try offenders before military courts
martial, rather than by regular civilian procedure. Only the
Okhrana, the secret police, fell outside his control. They com-
piled files on him and his staff and reported directly to the
Ministry of the Interior in Petersburg. As a liberal who admired
British constitutional monarchy, Paul disapproved of his own
arbitrary powers. But where were these powers set out? In the
Extraordinary and Temporary Measures of November 1881.
And who had been their draftsman? His own father.

Paul could not have been unaware of this irony, but he passed
it over in dutiful silence, as he passed over his father's anti-
Semitism. How was it between them at the end, the liberal son
who believed in guiding Russia slowly towards a constitutional
monarchy and the father who had known only the high noon of
autocracy? Did they ever broach their differences, when Paul
came down from Kiev to Kroupodernitsa to visit his father, when
he held the old man's arm as they walked along the avenue of
chestnut trees and sat on the benches there? There was the fault
line of their different temperaments: tempestuous old adventurer, cautious earnest son; there was the fault line of the times,
the father baffled by revolution, the son trying to navigate in the
storm. And there was the fault line of their age, a son coming into

his own at last, watching with mingled contempt and pity the rheumy decrepitude of a man whose shadow had loomed over his life so long. The silence was full between them as they sat side by side, father and son, on the sunlit bench.

The father's final years were grim: he had lost his youngest son to the sea in the battle of Tsushima in 1905 and he had lost his brother to an assassin's bullet in 1906. In 1908 his own time finally came. Paul buried his father in the family crypt beneath the village church in Kroupodernitsa; he ordered a black basalt monument on which were inscribed his father's name and rank, his dates, 1832–1908, and just the two names for his epitaph: Peking and San Stefano. He had lived too long and it had all slipped through his fingers, and when they buried him, in the village church, there was only the family to mourn him, led by his dry-eyed son.

No sooner had the body been laid to rest than the creditors began to descend. Grinevetsky, the swindling steward, shot himself on hearing of the old Count's death, and a crazy scheme of speculation which Grinevetsky had spun in the shelter of the old Count's name came tumbling out of locked cupboards and bank safes. With the governor's salary, his wife's dowry and the income from his estate, Paul silently set out to restore the family fortunes from the ruins. It took a decade.

However tawdry the actual inheritance, Paul always insisted that he had shouldered his father's legacy and traditions of service. He revered his father as an Asian empire-builder and triumphant diplomatist of the Turkish war and consigned to silence his fateful year as the anti-Semitic Minister of the Interior. When close friends like Vladimir Nabokov disposed of their court uniforms in protest at the unpunished pogroms of Kishinev and plunged into party politics, Paul could not follow them. Party politics was anathema to him, a betrayal of the oath of service he had given to the Tsar personally when serving in the Preobrajensky regiment during his military service. No matter that his father had been destroyed by service to the Tsar, no

[83]

matter that the regime of Nicholas II was increasingly unpalatable to liberals of his generation, Paul's life had meaning only within the terms of fidelity to his family's traditions of service. His life became a tortuous attempt to salvage what was honourable from what was reactionary in these traditions, to sustain their integrity at a historical moment which was breaking their meanings apart. While liberals of his generation chose to distance themselves from a regime ever more at odds with its own society, Paul chose to follow a path which took him to its very heart.

Through his work as governor of Kiev province, Paul had come to the attention of the Stolypin government in Petersburg, in particular to the attention of Krivoshein, the Minister of Agriculture, who invited the young governor to become head of the agriculture department in his ministry. It was a fateful move to the centre for someone who prided himself on being a man with soil on his boots, someone who kept his distance from the vortex of Petersburg intrigue. Natasha hated the idea, wanted to stay in her cosy Kiev and worried how she would manage in the cold and exalted Petersburg social atmosphere. But in the winter of 1908–09 the family moved to Petersburg, to a dark and narrow flat on Galernaya street just behind the quays near the Admiralty.

In the spring of 1909, to strengthen the children for the coming Petersburg winter, she took them all down to Eupatoria in the Crimea for a holiday. It is there that her son Alec's memory begins. He was three, wearing a sailor suit, sitting in a rowboat with a man in shirtsleeves. Suddenly the boat pitched over and Alec was tossed into the water. There were jellyfish in the water, Alec was screaming and the viscous, milky suckers were closing around him, the milky head pulsating, the tendrils billowing. He awakes now, a man in his late seventies, in the *terra incognita* between memory and nightmare.

There was typhoid at the resort, in the water supply, in the water ices the children ate on the terrace overlooking the sea, in the milk for the littlest one's formula. In two frightful hours,

Natasha watched Vladimir come down with the disease, and she saw the life of her youngest – Paul – ebb away before her eyes. In time she managed to speak of all her losses, all her dispossessions, but never this one, never the snuffing out of baby Paul's little life. How many times, in her most secret hours, must she have stalked that accursed ground in her memory wondering what else she might have done, how she might have deflected the falling sword. She never returned to the Crimea again, to those blessed estates of her childhood with the beautiful names – Koreis, Gaspra – but her memory must have marched her back again and again to that hotel bedroom in Eupatoria, to that empty cot. When the time finally came at the end of her life to put down what happened that summer of 1909, she did not write about it at all.

In her silence, I can sense what had been broken and could never be made right again. Paul had not been at the Crimea, he had not lived through those hours with her. He was days away by train in Petersburg, buried in his papers. Was it this, a fatal separation at a terrible hour, that dug the chasm between them, which meant that there was never the same consolation again in his embrace? Paul said only in his clenched way that 'in her anguish she gave all her attention to her remaining children and cut herself off increasingly from society.' He did not speak of his sorrow, but she withdrew behind the curtains to the solitude of a grieving heart. Through all the waystations of the life to come, she kept just one little picture in a round silver frame on her night table: the smiling image of her dead child.

FIVE

PETROGRAD

In the family album, there is a photograph of Natasha that dates
from the period when they came to live in Petersburg in the dark
and cluttered apartment on Galernaya street, two blocks from the
river Neva behind the English quay. She is dressed for a formal
winter evening, a fox fur draped over her shoulders, Brussels lace
on the bodice of her dark velvet gown, her hair swept back in a
tight chignon and a twelve-stranded pearl choker around her
stiffly upright neck. She is thin and pale, the cheekbones of her
long angular face taking the light, the eyes deep-set and dark.
Her expression is shy and guarded, and she seems at odds with
the occasion. Her hands are folded in her lap, the index finger of
her right hand curled tautly over her middle finger in a gesture of
concealment. She was a private soul: in the public glare, she
visibly shrank back. She hated Petersburg society: paying cour-
tesy calls on the wives of Paul's superiors, laying her calling card
on silver trays, making curtseys and small talk and all the while
feeling she was up on a high wire one step from a fall.

The photograph may be one of those taken by a court photographer during the celebrations held at the Winter Palace in
honour of the 300th anniversary of the Romanoff dynasty in
1913. If indeed this is the occasion, she had just passed through
the ritual of a presentation to the Empress. Masters of ceremonies in court uniforms, carrying tall gilded sticks, would sort
the society ladies by rank and form up processions to the throne,
each lady holding the train of the lady ahead. Natasha went with
her sister Sonia and they stood in line holding each other's train,
joking like schoolgirls until they were ushered forward and had to

curtsey quickly and move away before the ladies behind took their places. In the blur there was time only for an instant's glance at the glazed, frozen face of the Empress framed between glittering ropes of pearls that descended from her headdress. Immediately afterwards Natasha was ushered before the photographers set up in an adjacent room of the Winter Palace, and there in a puff of magnesium flare, she was fixed unblinking in the amber of another world.

On that evening in 1913 she was in her thirty-sixth year, mistress of a large household, wife of a rising star of the Petersburg bureaucracy, mother of 'four little wretches', Nicholas, Vladimir (Dima), Alec and Lionel. She was also expecting a fifth child, who was to be my father, George. In that blurred round of middle age, punctuated by the children's whooping coughs and typhoids, their winter colds and summer fevers, she watched half-aware as the ice formed at the heart of her marriage. In the bedroom, Paul now rose at seven and was assisted in his exercises, his ablutions and his dressing by Demian, his valet. While she remained in bed, he would breakfast downstairs with the children and their nannies. On busy mornings, Natasha remembered, 'he simply swallowed newspaper and breakfast and no end of phone calls,' and then hurried off down Galernaya street along the quays of the Neva to the Ministry of Agriculture. At seven he would return, bolt down his dinner and set to work on the portfolios brought to him by the office courier. And 'so till midnight', she remembered sadly, 'just work and every day for years the same routine'.

From the start, Paul was determined to resist becoming just another Petersburg bureaucrat. Within months of his arrival at the ministry, he had taken his fight to help the peasantry with loans, education and technical assistance right to meetings of Cabinet, while his own Minister, Krivoshein, tugged nervously at his coat-tails to make him sit down. When the Finance Minister muttered that Ignatieff's proposals smacked of Bismarckian state socialism, Paul replied that he preferred to experiment with state socialism rather than wait 'until the mob, which cannot understand where it is being led by the government, adopts its own simpler solutions and sweeps us away with all our culture'. An old admiral, representing the navy at the Cabinet, was so impressed that he offered the agriculture department expenditure credits worth half a battleship.

Natasha did her best to interest herself in his work, but could not share his worthy fascination with peasant land banks and credit schemes to enable small holders to purchase new machinery, the minutiae of his commitment to the liberalism of small deeds. When she tried to involve him in her life, a round of children's illnesses and endless petty struggles with the servants, his mind would stray back to his papers. In those moments when they were alone together, she shrank from him, either pregnant or recovering from pregnancy, unable to satisfy him, accumulating a weight of grief and guilt about their relations that burdened her heart until her last night alive. Of his own feelings about the widening gulf within their marriage, Paul never spoke.

Towards his sons Paul was an indulgent, if absent, father. He took his breakfast with them and read them items from his morning newspaper. When the *Titanic* went down, he read them the whole front page. On most days he let them walk with him to work, before they went back to their lessons with their tutors in the schoolroom of the apartment. He was back again at night for prayers and then in the summer holidays he took them sailing in the Baltic. On one of these holidays at a 'mucky' (Natasha's word) German resort called Misdroy, a picture was taken of the family standing in the sand in front of a cane and canvas beach hut. The boys are in ankle boots and sailor suits. Lionel, still a baby, is making a crazy face in the arms of a stout, brown-faced nursemaid while Paul has his arm around Dima, who leans against his father. Paul is wearing a cloth cap in honour of the holiday and he is whistling through his moustache, with a vague, happy expression on his face. He looks as if he is about to buy them all ice cream.

Natasha is wearing a high white blouse fastened at the neck, underneath a full-length travelling coat, and she looks happy and relaxed, her hand resting on little Nicholas's shoulder. Next to her stands a small round-faced black-haired girl in a white servant's uniform. She was Tonia, the eldest boys' nursery maid, and next to her stands a new arrival in the family, a firm-jawed and unsmiling Englishwoman of twenty-one called Peggy Meadowcroft.

In 1912, Natasha applied to an agency in London for a governess. The three eldest boys, by then eight, seven and six, were cadging cigarettes from the cab drivers on the corners and getting into fights. They were becoming more than either Natasha or a succession of nannies could handle, and the boys were demanding that if they had to have a nanny at all, she had better be a pretty one for a change. In due course a stern, fair-skinned girl with golden hair in a broad Edwardian straw hat, a lace choker and a white high-waisted dress arrived with her suitcases at the house on Galernaya. Paul took one look at her and announced, 'Now hooliganism will be controlled.'

Hooliganism was most emphatically controlled. Peggy Meadowcroft, beneath her fey and feminine straw hats, turned out to be a redoubtable Edwardian adventuress from the lower middle class, armoured with a brisk sense of British cultural superiority. The reign of old Russian chaos was ended. From the beginning, she gave everyone a piece of her mind: the boys for their dirty ears and messy writing, the ladies' maids for their slovenly way with a tucked-in corner, the cooks for the sloppy unpunctuality of her meals. She quickly learned to speak a Russian that surrendered nothing to the accents of Putney. The boys, now edging towards adolescence, were dazzled by her good looks, whispered together under the covers about what they saw when she was wearing that translucent nightie of hers, and watched open-mouthed as she waded into Russian life. When she took them out on walks and came across some old broken-down cab driver beating his horse, she did not hesitate for an instant. Waving her brolly, she would stride across the street and bring the descending whip to a halt in mid-air as she shouted in her high-pitched Putney Russian. The boys would stand on the icy quay, watching the crowd gather and not knowing whether to burn with shame or glow with pride. Natasha was guarded and correct with Peggy, irritated with her 'bored stiff look' and her humourless bustle. As a wife, she watched the glances that Peggy began casting in her husband's direction and the glances that were returned. Among the photos Peggy took of a family holiday in Switzerland in the hills above Lausanne, during the summer of 1913, there is one reverently labelled Count Paul, of him standing in an alpine meadow, leaning jauntily on a walking stick, knapsack over his shoulder, smiling broadly beneath his moustaches. His gaze seems to bask in hers. They must have gone walking in the mountains alone together. In the same album, there is one of Natasha back at the Grand Hôtel Muverand heavily pregnant, sitting in a wicker chair in the hotel garden, wearing a broad-brimmed hat to keep the sun off her face. She is holding on to a walking stick to help her keep her balance. Peggy has asked her to pose and Natasha's averted gaze flickers with a sense of invaded privacy.

The light in the photograph is the pale, bleached glow of autumn, a season that filled Natasha with melancholy. She stayed on with the boys after Paul returned to Petersburg, and the Grand Hôtel Muverand stayed open just for them. She felt heavy and wretched. It was the season of the grape harvest. The vines on the hillside below the hotel were loaded with swollen grapes. She sat on the terrace in the sun trying to gather her strength.

George, my father, was born in the bedroom of 67 Galernaya in Petersburg in December 1913, a child with curly auburn hair – an Ignatieff rather than a Mestchersky in the round fullness of his face, the only one of her children, she thought, who really looked like his father. He cried solidly for six weeks, and when placed in the baptismal font held on to his blanket with a grip no one could loosen. At the baptism, the family priest Father Nicholas placed around his neck a gold cross given him by his grandmother Ignatieff, which he wears to this day.

He arrived into the family just as its fortunes were about to take a dramatic turn. Early in 1914, Paul was named joint heir of the Maltsev industrial empire. Yuri Nechaev Maltsev, an old bachelor, had built up one of the largest industrial fortunes in Russia. His factories southwest of Moscow were one of the pistons driving that frantic industrialization which made Russia the world's fastest-growing economy before the First World War. Cotton from the American South funnelled through Liverpool was turned into cloth and thread in two of the factories, while other plants turned out everything from thermometers to cement. Over 20,000 workmen worked in these factories and lived in a Pullman-type industrial town under the benevolent despotism of old man Maltsev. The women gave birth in his hospitals, their children went to his schools and on Sunday they prayed in his church.

A man without education himself, Maltsev had a reverence for learning and when Ivan Tsevetaev was seeking a patron to support his project of a museum to house Moscow University's collection of plaster replicas of Egyptian, Greek and Roman antiquities, it was Maltsev who found him the money. The shrivelled multimillionaire was there leaning on his cane on the grand morning in May 1912 when Nicholas II inaugurated the Museum of Fine Arts in Moscow – now the Pushkin Museum – built with his benefactions.

Maltsev was a lonely man who gave elaborate Christmas parties for the Ignatieff boys and who showered all the family with gifts on weddings and anniversaries, even though the family connection between the Maltsevs and Ignatieffs was indirect. Paul was stunned when the lawyers broke the seal on Maltsev's will and announced – to general amazement – that he was to be Maltsev's heir. There was just one catch. Paul inherited the factories themselves, while a friend and relative, Prince Demidoff, inherited the capital.

Everyone in Petersburg expected the new heir to take his retirement from the Ministry of Agriculture and become an industrial baron. But to the family tradition, trade and industry were interesting hobbies but not serious vocations. State service remained the only conceivable path. Paul established a limited company and appointed a Baltic German named Schlippe to run the place in his name.

There had always been money in the Ignatieff family, but now for the first time there were real riches. Nothing dramatic or ostentatious was done with the money: Prince Demidoff had the capital, and besides, ostentation was frowned upon. Still, a *dacha* could be rented in fashionable Tsarskoe Selo so that the boys could escape the summer fevers of Petersburg and play in the royal parks; there was a new Renault to take Paul on the hour-long journey between Tsarskoe Selo and his office; a search began for a new house; and most of all, family honour could be rebuilt: father's debts could be paid off. With black humour and inimitable timing, Fortune had decided to shine on the family at just the moment everything was about to be swept away.

In August 1914, the family was at Vybiti, the country house of Natasha's older sister Sonia and her husband Boria Wassiltchikoff, two hours' drive from Petersburg. The house rang with the sounds of children. Nick, Dima and Alec played with their beautiful Galitzine cousins from Novgorod. In the photographs the girls are all wearing bright floral pinafores and floppy white hats against the sun. The boys are in sailor suits with short pants and straw boaters. The hot August fields of Vybiti stretched on to the curve of the horizon line. The poplars lining the long drives flickered with sunlight. At the top of the curve of a gravel driveway stood the great house, a dark green vine twined around the columned entrance. The photographs from that holiday are full of small happy faces out of focus. The little girls are beautiful, their long hair twined in lustrous braids tied with little blue ribbons. Of all those August afternoons Dima and Alec remember the one when they sneaked away from their sleeping parents and crept through the high grass, to lie crouching by the riverbank where they could see the girls splashing knee-deep and unaware in the brown river stream, their hats and pinafores strewn on the grass bank.

Then suddenly the boys' tutors were standing on the porch reading the day's papers to crowds of villagers gathered in the driveway: news about the death of an archduke in a Bosnian street, exchanges of diplomatic notes and sombre declarations from important statesmen with foreign names. The peasants with memories of the Russo-Japanese War grumbled while their sons hurried to enlist. Natasha and her sister Sonia handed sweets and small packets of money to the recruits who assembled in companies on the driveway in front of the big house. They watched as they marched off, their 'brave elastic step' raising a cloud of summer dust down the long poplar alleys.

When everyone had gone, when the nursemaids and tutors had gathered up all the children and had taken them back to Petersburg, Natasha stayed alone at Vybiti and had the echoing sunny rooms to herself. She savoured that lingering September, gripped by a presentiment that she would never enjoy such peace again.

By the time she returned to the capital, its name had been changed to Petrograd to give it a more Russian, less German sound. The wounded were beginning to be brought from the front to the hospital ward established by her husband's department in one of the exhibition halls of the Petersburg agricultural museum. Twice a week, she took the train down from the family's rented *dacha* in Tsarskoe Selo to type letters for the soldiers. With a black Imperial portable poised on her knee, she would sit beside the men and ask them what she should type. The peasants all began their letters with 'endless sorts of bows and salutations' to the village elders, the priest and their relations. But when it came to what they should say about their wounds or their hopes the men would look up at her and say, 'Write what you think best.'

They asked her for little things: Bibles, harmonicas, a pair of gloves for a girlfriend. One blind boy wanted a concertina to play now that he could no longer see. She sat and watched the life slip away from their waxen faces.

Paul's sister Katia was running a hospital train on the Polish front somewhere near Lodz; Aunt Mika had turned a wing of the house at Kroupodernitsa into a hospital for recruits from the village; Paul's brother Kolya was leading the Preobrajensky Guards into battle on the Polish plains; another of Paul's brothers, Leonid, was a Cossack general on the southwestern front. The war began drawing the family towards its hearth.

In January 1915, Paul was requested to present himself at Nicholas II's residence at Tsarskoe Selo. The Agriculture Minister, Krivoshein, in search of liberal allies in the Cabinet, had proposed to the Tsar that Paul be chosen to replace a reactionary Minister of Education who had just died. Paul presented himself to the sovereign and was surprised and flattered to hear Nicholas recalling the conversation they had had together, nearly twenty years before, over coffee in Paul's tent at Gatchina during regimental manoeuvres of the Preobrajensky Guards. Did Count Ignatieff recall what he had said about the autocracy of the scribe, the clerk, the policeman, the governor, and even the minister, the Tsar asked evenly. It was a disarming gambit and Paul, who had been approached once before for ministerial office and had declined, left the interview as Minister of Education.

The Tsar's eerie feat of memory fostered the illusion in Paul that the sovereign would always heed the words of honest men. This illusion drew Paul into the heart of a regime that both right and left circles in Petrograd regarded as beyond help. At the salons of his aunt, the widow of his uncle Alexis, the assassinated governor of Tver, the talk was openly contemptuous of Nicholas II's weakness and vacillation, while among Paul's friends in the Kadet Party, men like Vladimir Nabokov believed the only salvation of the country lay in the establishment of a democratic republic. Yet Paul himself, aware as anyone else of Nicholas's feeble intelligence and puppyish dependence on his wife, retained a mystical reverence for the office of Tsar as spiritual father of his people. Here he let himself be betrayed by the Slavophile family traditions, by the belief that if the bureaucratic wall dividing Tsar from people could be broken down Russia could chart a middle course between despotism and republicanism in its encounter with modernity. It was on such traditions of service that his very identity was built. Family traditions made him and family traditions drew him under.

He set out to make the Russian school curriculum less remote and scholastic, closer to the needs of agriculture and industry, and instead he found himself struggling to maintain teachers' ranks despite the steady haemorrhage to the front; he wanted to create a single unified system of popular education open to all with advancement based on merit; and he found himself arguing with Cabinet colleagues over whether Jewish children chased out of the western Pale by military authorities could enrol in Gentile schools. He wanted the school to be the centre of village life, to be a community centre rather than a barracks; instead, as the terrible retreats of 1915 began, he was organizing the use of schools as dormitories for refugees. He wanted to free the schools from the grip of useless examinations and to enlarge vocational training; with each succeeding month more school districts in the western provinces had to be evacuated. He sought to defend the autonomy of the universities from government interference and found instead that the Tsarina insisted on making appointments to the Petrograd University staff.

The Cabinet, chaired by I. L. Goremikin, a man he regarded as a senile incompetent, was so bitterly divided that some members left the room when others began to speak. It had no jurisdiction over military matters, no collective policy, not even a shared doctrine of Cabinet responsibility. Each minister was responsible to the Tsar alone; like the others, Paul put on his court uniform every month or so and journeyed out to Tsarskoe Selo to make a personal report to the sovereign; and like the others he was free to criticize – and often did so – the decisions taken collectively at Cabinet. At the same time, Cabinet decisions were often reversed by the Tsar. As the months passed, Paul came to understand with increasing despair that the institution of autocracy itself was incapable of running a modern war.

He tried as a minister to secure the cooperation of the Russian parliament, the Duma, going to its sittings at the Tauride Palace in person to present and defend his estimates against the attack from the right wing only to find that other ministers refused to recognize the Duma's authority. As an old veteran of the *zemstvo* movement, Paul took the *zemstvos* into his confidence and then had to listen in Cabinet while his colleagues talked about them as if they were subversive organizations. Above all, he was aware that power was slipping away from the Cabinet table – to military headquarters at Mogilev, to the Empress's suite in Tsarskoe Selo, and worst of all to the Petrograd salons presided over by the sexually rapacious and mentally disordered monk Grigori Rasputin. It was galling to know that one of these salons was held in the house of his aunt, wife of his assassinated uncle Alexis. There the monk enjoyed his visions in the company of reactionary hysterics.

Paul sat silently through Cabinet discussions which took on an increasingly grotesque and surreal character. As the Russian army fell back, driving before them the wretched *shtetl* Jews of the northeastern plains of Poland and Russia, the Cabinet spent hours debating whether to abolish restrictions on Jewish settlement in towns just as the brutal arbitrage of war consigned the paraphernalia of restriction to oblivion. Minister after minister accepted as part of their mental universe that the international Jewish banking elite had imperial Russia at its mercy: some thought it best to abolish the restrictions to placate the bankers, others thought it indecent that the autocracy should have to bow to Jewish money. Paul kept silent during these fantastic discussions but went privately to the Tsar to plead that restrictions on

Jewish admission to schools outside the Pale be removed. The Tsar refused, allowing him only to establish all-Jewish private schools for evacuees from Pale areas. Occasionally he was able to put a spoke in the wheel of prejudice. When the police arrived at the officers' hospital in Tsarskoe Selo to take custody of a decorated veteran because he was a Jew and thus not allowed to recover outside the Pale, he enrolled the boy in Petrograd University, thus granting him the right to remain in his hospital bed.

As the western front collapsed, as peasant recruits armed at times only with bayonets crawled out of their trenches and retreated back through Poland, the War Minister told his colleagues, 'I rely on impassable spaces, on impenetrable mud and on the mercy of St Nicholas, the patron of Holy Russia.' From his brother Kolya, Paul heard about the rout at Tannenberg, and the Cabinet began to understand how fatally wrong they had been to suppose the war would last no more than a year. He himself remembered Cabinet meetings when the Finance Minister had rejected plans to build domestic munitions factories on the grounds that foreign supplies would be adequate. Now the troops at the front lacked cartridges, shoes, blankets, even uniforms. The scandal cost the War Minister his job. In Paris, Paul's cousin Alyosha, the Russian military attaché, was frantically buying arms from the French munition plants at Le Creusot.

Then the war struck home. Paul's sister Katia contracted an infection while kneeling in the filthy straw, nursing soldiers in a hospital train near Lodz. A blood clot formed and passed into her lungs. In two days she was dead. Paul went by ministerial train to Warsaw to collect the body. He accompanied it across Russia to the little station near Kroupodernitsa, where the peasant elders unloaded the coffin from the train and took turns bearing it down the two miles of muddy road to the crypt beneath the village church. There, her mother watched as her daughter was laid to rest in the family vault.

At Easter 1915, Paul brought the whole family down to

Kroupodernitsa to be with his mother, to draw on her strength and reassurance. When the Kiev–Odessa express with the minister's private sleeper pulled up at the little family station, carriages were waiting for the family down a long flight of wooden steps from the railway embankment. Grooms were standing at the top and bottom of the steps with flaming pitch torches to light their way. They sped off, the coachmen snapping their whips and the horses galloping into the darkness. As they drew up before the house, grandmother Ignatieff was waiting for them on the veranda, swathed in a white shawl. She held each of her grandchildren's faces in her hands and kissed them on their foreheads.

At the Easter midnight service the church was packed with villagers in sheepskin coats which gave the air a pungent acrid smell. Grandmother Ignatieff made sure her grandchildren stood up straight and poked them sharply if one of them slouched or leaned against a pillar. The church was dark and sombre until the moment when the verger lit the first candle in the chandelier. The light coursed along the network of braided wicks until the whole church was ablaze with tiny flames and the walls resounded with the cry, 'Christ is risen! Christ is risen indeed!' Everyone carried his own lighted candle too, and as the villagers dispersed back into the night, they shielded their candles with cupped hands, and the fields and lanes were aglow with hundreds of departing figures etched in fragile light.

Peggy Meadowcroft's album is full of pictures from that Easter at the estate: the thatched cottages of the village, the family retainers, Sessoueff and Rudnitsky, standing stiffly beneath the tree in the dusty village square with their children and barefoot wives ranged around them; Vassilieff, the groom, with two new foals; a giant pair of oxen in the paddock; young Nicholas astride his favourite mare, Narzan; a choir feast outdoors in the woods after the Easter services, the trestle tables piled with braided bread, wooden spoons and soup, the men singers at one table, the women in costume at another, and grandmother Ignatieff and

Paul strolling from table to table. There are many photographs of grandmother Ignatieff, always wreathed in shawls, with her grandchildren at her side. There is a serenity about her now. She seems less austere and formidable than she had been when Natasha first knew her. Her grandchildren crowd around affectionately: she smells sweet, her hands are gentle. In the garden, holding Lionel on her knee, she smiles benignly, the melancholy beauty who had caught Disraeli's eye now entering her seventy-third year.

In one of Peggy Meadowcroft's pictures, Paul is standing beside a file of wounded soldiers convalescing in his sister Mika's hospital established in a wing of the house. He is wearing a tail coat, striped pants, wing collar and tie, with an astrakhan perched jauntily on the back of his head. He is standing at attention with his hands down the creases of his trousers. He is smiling. Beside him stand the soldiers, one on crutches, another with a bandaged arm, another with the white gauze of a dressing showing at the neck. They are not smiling.

At Bossibrod station after that Easter vacation of 1915, the great engine poured gushers of steam into the night, and the boys sat in the ministerial carriage, a cube of light in the Ukrainian darkness, and looked back at their grandmother waving them goodbye from that little station platform. They never saw her again.

As the train swept northwards towards Petrograd, there would have been ragged columns of swathed figures, visible at the edge of the lights from the carriages, carrying bundles, their feet wrapped in sacking against the cold, trudging away from the front. Other trains besides theirs, military trains bearing the detritus of swiftly evacuated army headquarters, would blast past them and at the windows monocled faces would scratch at the frost and stare at these passing processions of wraiths, these numb, exhausted people who were soon to be their judges.

When the family returned to Petrograd rumours were sweeping the city of German invasion armies landing on the Baltic coast. The ascendancy of Rasputin's clique at court made the impotence of Cabinet discussions more and more humiliating. In August 1915 the Tsar decided to take over personal command of the army from his uncle Grand Duke Nicholas. Paul was appalled. The decision meant that if there were further disasters at the front, the Tsar himself would be blamed and the autocracy itself would be in danger. Paul's friend the Agriculture Minister Krivoshein warned the Cabinet, which had not been advised or consulted about the Tsar's decision, that the country was 'rolling down the hill not only towards a military but towards an internal catastrophe'. The secret Cabinet minutes of August 1915 record Paul as observing dryly that the army was ceasing to be an army, and in the rout had become 'a people in arms'. The students at the universities, he reported, were joining the industrial demonstrations and disorders which had begun in Moscow and Petrograd. Hearing rumours of an invasion from the Baltic, he drew up contingency plans for the evacuation of libraries and schools in the capital itself.

At a Cabinet meeting at Tsarskoe Selo, Paul and seven other Cabinet ministers begged Nicholas II not to take command of the army. On their return to the capital, the dissident ministers, including Paul, signed a joint letter of resignation, warning the Tsar that his decision threatened Russia and the dynasty. The Tsar, unmoved, boarded his train for the front. A month later the Cabinet was ordered to appear at the headquarters where the Tsar appealed to them to work together. Goremikin, the Prime Minister, seconded the Tsar's appeal to them by 'calling on them to work as the old Russian nobility had always worked – not because of fear, but for conscience sake'. Paul was outraged that their courage had been impugned. The meeting ended with the Tsar's curt dismissal of them. On the return journey by train to the capital, Paul and his colleagues sat in shaken silence.

Days later, Paul was received at Tsarskoe Selo by the Empress, dressed in a nurse's uniform. When she appealed to him to work with Goremikin, Paul replied that events had passed beyond saving by any one man. The army could no longer be trusted against the populace; the old regiments had fallen on the fields of Galicia, Poland and East Prussia. The only solution was a government 'leaning on organized society' working in union with the 'social forces of the country' to mobilize those who have 'something to lose from disorder'. This meant a Cabinet that would enforce collective responsibility and seek support from the Duma for its measures. She could see as clearly as Paul that this would mean the end of the autocracy and the establishment of a constitutional monarchy. Her reply closed every door: 'The Tsar cannot yield. He will only be asked to surrender something more. Where will it end? What power will be left the Tsar?'

Everywhere in Russia, she went on, the humble people had rallied to her husband, except in the Cabinet and among the discontented rabble of the cities. In the countryside the People, that holy abstraction, were behind their Tsar. The irony was that her views, which filled Paul with despair, were a parody of his own: the Tsar was separated from his people; he must draw closer to them. So when the Tsar decided to take command of the army, to make himself one with a people in arms, Paul found his liberal convictions impaled on the contradiction between his commitment to the personal autocracy of the Tsar and an essentially British ideal of constitutional government.

The Empress stood stiffly throughout their interview. After forty-five minutes she concluded tersely, 'Doubtless you know what is done with a regiment when anything occurs between the commanders and its officers such as what has happened in the Cabinet. It is disbanded.'

'It is what we are praying for,' was Paul's answer.

By the autumn of 1915, the losses at the front had been stemmed, and with the immediate crisis past, the Tsar no longer felt bound to conciliate public opinion with the inclusion of liberal figures like Krivoshein. Five of the other ministers who had opposed the Tsar's decision to take command of the army were sacked. The Empress had marked Paul down as a dangerous liberal, yet to everyone's surprise, he was one of three members of the Cabinet to be retained. He begged the Tsar to be relieved of his post. He was told that 'the faithful defenders do not desert the trenches' and so he soldiered on at the Ministry of Education. By the autumn of 1915, he was the last Russian liberal at the heart of the regime.

The Tsar apparently kept him because he had a soft spot for old regimental companions. Perhaps too he responded to that mysticism of service in which the young minister continued to define his obligations to a dying regime. At his next audience with the Tsar Paul stated his personal credo:

'I am neither a politician nor a bureaucrat. I am only a citizen, and as a citizen I look at the problems of life and seek to solve them from the point of view of the average man living in Russia and his interests, which properly understood do not differ at all from the interest of the state. Not only shall I always remain a citizen of Russia, but I shall stand firmly on the tradition of my family, which includes acceptance of the principle of the union between the Tsar and his people, transcending the partition wall created by bureaucratic interests.'

The Tsar in his wooden way remarked that he had often reiterated the same point of view. When Paul pleaded for the Tsar to name a ministry that would have the confidence of the progressive bloc of the Fourth Duma and the *zemstvo* movement, the Tsar replied with the duplicity of the weak, 'You shall see.' The Tsar then replaced Goremikin with another nonentity whose only recommendation was the Tsarina's support. Paul tendered his resignation again but was ordered by the Tsar to remain 'in the trenches at Tschernischeff Bridge', the site of the Ministry of Education.

Through the winter of 1916, Paul remained at his post, isolated, divided within himself, ever more exhausted by the struggle to run an education service in a regime staggering towards collapse. The Cabinet note-taker recorded that in moments of stress the Minister of Education would run his hands through his sparse remaining hair with a kind of convulsive motion. He said less and less in Cabinet. The meetings were a farce. He was bypassed by a kitchen Cabinet which took such decisions as there were still to take: they delayed the opening of Petrograd schools in the autumn of 1916 without even informing him; huge sums to bribe the press were slipped past the Cabinet, despite his personal protest to the Tsar. When he pleaded against the Cabinet decision to switch the control of provisioning from the Ministry of Agriculture to the Ministry of the Interior, he concluded his monthly audience with the Tsar with the words: 'It needs only a spark to cause a terrible conflagration.' The Tsar, withdrawn inside a rigid calm, replied softly that everything seemed worse in Petrograd than it actually was. Both men now, Tsar and minister, were in hallucinatory stages of exhaustion. During audiences, the Emperor gazed out of the window, a look of mute Byzantine suffering already etched on his face, while his minister went through the motions of a report in a stumbling monotone. Through the year of 1916, Paul slowly came apart.

There are no pictures of him during this period. He had been swept out of the family frame altogether by the final convulsions of the regime. Peggy Meadowcroft's album is full of pictures of George, aged two and a half, in a white smock and button shoes, holding a tennis racquet or riding his tricycle in the garden of the family *dacha* in Tsarskoe Selo. There are pictures of the boys skiing in the woods and across the frozen lakes of the Tsarskoe Selo park. Everyone smiles easily: only the light – of autumn 1916 – is dark behind.

That autumn Natasha's sister, Sonia Wassiltchikoff, dashed off a note to the Empress – begging her to keep out of politics and to cease to listen to Rasputin. She thought, naively, that she could write informally, woman to woman. Punishment was swift: immediate banishment to their estate at Vybiti; dismissal of her husband from his ceremonial functions at court.

In October 1916, Natasha gave birth prematurely to a baby boy. They placed him in an incubator and called a priest, who christened him Alexander. She lay in bed and heard his weak snuffling cries in the next room and then in her weakness, half way between sleep and waking, she recognized Father Nicholas's voice next door intoning the prayers for the dying. The child died that night. The little casket was placed in the vault of a church in Tsarskoe Selo until the time came to take it down to the family vault at Kroupodernitsa. She believed that God had taken him into his mighty arms to spare him the future that groaned and creaked up ahead like the ice under the Neva bridges.

The bitter Petrograd winter came on: darkness fell in the early afternoon, and the wind howled along the quays at dusk. At dawn the city was enveloped in freezing fog. Now stones were hurled out of the darkness at the Ignatieffs' car when they drove into the city.

In November 1916 Paul attended his last Cabinet meeting, convened to consider a response to a motion in the Duma accusing the Cabinet of treason. The Prime Minister lay at one end of a dark and gloomy room, stretched out in an armchair, nursing a gouty foot. All possible stratagems were rejected one after the other. After a long silence, the Prime Minister looked at Paul and said in a dismal voice, 'Count, you help us.' Angrily, Paul answered: 'I am kept in this Cabinet against my will. It has become clear that this Cabinet does not dare, has not the moral standing to enter into negotiations with the State Duma or the country.' He said he would not approach the Duma as a representative of the Cabinet, but solely in a personal capacity. When one of the Cabinet members wanted to know what their 'delegate' proposed to say, Paul declared angrily, 'It seems to me that I have not been understood. I cannot and do not wish to be a delegate and I shall not give any account of my actions here. If these conditions are not acceptable I shall not move a finger.'

They allowed him one last try to reach an accord with the Duma. But when he had succeeded in negotiating a softening of the Duma's language, he discovered that the Minister of the Interior, Protopopoff, had circulated a rumour to the effect that recalcitrant Duma members would be conscripted for service in the trenches if they passed the original motion. The last chance of reconciliation between government and Duma – if it had ever been a real chance at all – had been sabotaged. Several nights later, the Duma leader Miliukov made a speech whose indictment of the Cabinet rang at the end of every paragraph, 'Is this stupidity or is it treason?'

Paul journeyed out to headquarters once more in the ministerial train. He pointed out to the Tsar that Protopopoff had made a public statement to the effect that the army had food supplies for four years. 'What else can this be described as other than a crime?' he asked. 'If it is so, why are the people standing in queues half starved? What else is it than an effort to provoke the people against the army?' Again the Tsar answered, 'Thank you. Now my eyes are opened. Stay and work for my sake.' Paul was told to report next morning for a further audience. Paul went the rounds of headquarters pleading with everyone to persuade the Tsar to remove Protopopoff. One of the generals shrugged his shoulders: '*Vous plaidez une cause perdue.*' That night Paul was trying to sleep in his ministerial train in a siding of the little country station at Mogilev when his carriage shook to the passage of an express drawing into the station. Looking through the blinds, he could see that the Tsarina had arrived and that the Tsar had gone immediately to her train.

Next morning Paul waited in vain for a summons to the promised audience with the Tsar. At lunch, he watched, with a dawning comprehension, as the Tsar and Tsarina entered, failed to acknowledge his greeting and turned their backs on the cluster of ministers standing at the end of the room. Other officers and Cabinet officials were presented to the Tsarina. He stood apart, aware that she had decided his fate. Two days later he returned for an audience, with a letter of resignation in his hand. He read it to the Tsar in a hoarse and strained voice:

Your Imperial Majesty and Most Gracious Sovereign:

On November 19, at the headquarters of your Majesty, I felt it to be a duty to state that my conscience and my oath of office made it necessary for me to report the apprehensions which cause me concern about the acts of certain persons and the trend of the political life of the country. I implored your Imperial Majesty not to force me to be an accomplice of those persons, whose acts my conscience warned me were ruinous to the throne and the fatherland. In the firm conviction that only a government united in the necessity of the unity of the State, with a common understanding of the fundamental goals of government and of the way in which these can be achieved, can be of any use to your Imperial Majesty and the fatherland. I esteem it my duty as a loyal subject humbly to beg your Imperial Majesty to relieve me from the unbearable burden of serving contrary to the dictates of my conscience.

I beg you to believe, my Sovereign, that I am forced to petition you for this gracious act, by the traditions inherited from my ancestors, tried by centuries of faithfulness to the immemorial principles on which the might of the Russian State was founded and which has rested on the union of the Tsar with his people.

Even when separated from a direct share in the conduct of affairs in accordance with the principles and examples set by my father, I shall remain the same loyal servant of your Majesty, the throne and the fatherland.

Your Imperial Majesty's loyal subject and servant Equerry Count Paul Ignatieff.

After a moment of silence, the Tsar lifted his eyes and said, 'Do not be agitated. Go on with your useful work. Your petition will remain with me in my desk.' With these words he opened a drawer in the table and put the petition into it.

That evening Paul learned from a newspaperman friend that he had been replaced as minister. He made the final round of the ministry. His subordinates assembled in the great hall and they exchanged words of deep feeling. They asked him to speak, but the words would not come and he stood in silence, blinking. He could recall only a line from a poem: 'Friends, row hard, row hard.' They carried him on their shoulders down the steps of the ministry to his car.

He was summoned to Tsarskoe Selo for a farewell audience. Rasputin's body had been found floating in the Neva that morning. The Tsar scarcely seemed to be listening to him when Paul said, 'It was the mercy of God.' Awakened from his reverie, the Tsar looked at him sharply: 'You mean, the will of God.' 'No, your Majesty, I mean the mercy of God. It might have finished worse.' Paul said he wished he could have remained to continue the work he had started, to which the Tsar replied, 'Do not be afraid. I stay here and guard all that you have done.' He then added in a quiet distant voice: 'You told me the truth,' and after a pause, 'as you saw it.' With these words the Tsar clasped him in his arms, and said, 'Go to your mother now; take a rest, restore your health and return to go on with your work.' In tears, Paul answered, 'Your Majesty, something tells me that I shall never again be in this room. May God protect you.'

SIX

REVOLUTION

'**G**o to your mother' had been the Tsar's last words. After his final audience with the Tsar, Paul travelled down to Kroupodernitsa to be with his mother. In the crypt of the village church they sang the *pannihida*, the memorial service for the dead, on the anniversary of his father's death. They stood together, mother and son, in the low vaulted crypt lit by the icon lamps, and on the black basalt tomb the inscription 'Peking and San Stefano' gleamed like a scar.

Paul had been a liberal constitutional monarchist, his father a defender of autocracy: both had gone under, at fifty, at the height of their powers, cast away by a regime they had tried to serve. They were too much alike, too much of one flesh, for Paul to escape the same fatal unwinding, the inner dissolution that had befallen his father. The coils of energy, will and motive wound tight for fifteen years began to unravel.

While the wind whistled across the bare fields, Paul sat with his mother on the sofa in the sitting room at Kroupodernitsa, opening more than 3000 letters and telegrams which arrived at the estate once his dismissal was announced. The *zemstvo* movement told him his work would not be forgotten and teachers' unions from Smolensk to Vladivostok sent him messages of support.

The church choir had prepared a performance of extracts from Glinka's *A Life for the Tsar*, and they asked Paul to sing a solo part. The concert was given in the sitting room of the big house. His mother, matriarch of the village, swathed in white shawls, sat by the fire with Paul's sister Mika beside her. Around them were ranged the village elders, the head of the fire brigade and the priest, and against the walls stood the servants who had taught Paul to ride and hunt and fish – Mitro, Sessoueff, Rudnitsky and Vassilieff, together with their wives and children. Still more villagers stood outside, their faces against the veranda windows. Everyone sang the patriotic choruses, and then they listened while their master sang the solo, which they cheered and made him repeat. It was called 'In The Storm'.

Paul stayed with his mother for six weeks and returned to the capital in mid-February 1917. On his way back from the station in Petrograd, he passed detachments of Siberian Cossacks on their small shaggy ponies, champing and pawing the frozen ground of the private courtyards in the streets near his home. Machine-gun nests were going up on the rooftops of public buildings.

By then the family had moved into a big house on Fourstatskaya street, a block away from the Tauride Palace where the Duma held its sittings. It was in a leafy and substantial district where the fashionable regiments had their barracks and fashionable people had their mansions. Theirs was a three-storey edifice with Corinthian columns around the windows and large iron gates guarding the driveway. Built as the Spanish embassy in the 1890s, it was decorated in the florid style of Spanish baroque. After Paul bought it in 1915, builders were brought in to tone down some of the Spanish extravagance and to take the fountain out of the sitting room. In December 1916, the family moved from the rented *dacha* in Tsarskoe Selo in a chaotic procession of motorcars and trucks. Paul, by then at the end of his tether, left Natasha, herself exhausted from the birth and death of her baby, to supervise the move.

It was a coldly official residence that defeated Natasha's efforts to make it a family home. There was a doorman standing at the mahogany doors and two little messenger boys in blue coats waiting in the marble hallway outside the master study, a gloomy leather sanctum to which the children were not admitted. The hallway, laid out in black and white marble squares, led between two marble pillars to a chandelier-lit double stairway that curved upstairs to the ballroom, sitting room, dining rooms and bedrooms. These heavy formal rooms, with their *trompe l'oeil* cherubs and grey and white plaster mouldings, were not the place for toys, for hide-and-seek or for card games on the carpets. Family life withdrew upstairs to the warren of little white rooms where the children slept and the servants had their quarters.

Twenty-eight people slept under that roof in February 1917: Paul and Natasha and their five boys; two nursery maids; Roman, the Polish footman; three serving maids; Koulakoff, the Cossack butler; Demian, Paul's valet; Natasha's maid, Katia; the yardman, or *dvornik*, and the stoveman; the two errand boys and the doorman; Basil, the chauffeur; a charlady; two Ukrainian scullery maids and a large placid cook; and, in rooms of their own at the back, Peggy Meadowcroft and the boys' French tutor, Monsieur Darier.

The rhythm of the household was measured and quiet, cocooned in warmth and comfort. In the cellar, the stoveman stoked the furnace; Basil fetched the milk churns from the station every morning and the yardman rolled them to the pantry door; the ladies' maids took up the breakfasts on trays; Koulakoff woke the eldest boys and supervised the washing of their hands and faces; Demian handed his master his clothes; Darier paced the downstairs classroom and the older boys did dictations from the pages of Anatole France or Sainte-Beuve while the younger ones, swaddled in furs, were taken out in their perambulators; Roman pulled on his white gloves and served lunch; the scullery maids peeled the potatoes; the doorman opened the door to let the boys in with their toboggans from the Tauride Park; the little messenger boys waited outside the study door for their master's messages; and at night the hooves of the Cossack ponies pawed the packed snow of the courtyard across the street. Natasha tossed in her bed trying to sleep and upstairs Nicholas, her eldest son, sat by his bedroom window watching the northern lights in the sky.

On a bright morning in late February, the boys were having their lessons when they heard a truck swerve past the house, followed by another and still another. When they peeked through the curtains, soldiers and women were standing in the back of the trucks shouting and waving guns. Monsieur Darier stopped his dictation and joined the boys at the window. He heard a wisp of a song caught on the winter air. 'The Marseillaise!' he cried. 'The Marseillaise. Hurrah!' he shouted, looking more excited than they had ever seen him. He thought the troops in the trucks were celebrating a victory on the western front.

When the firing began in the neighbouring streets, they thought it might be just the police putting down some strikes. But then, like a river bed overrun by a flash flood, the street filled with a grey-coloured torrent of soldiers, streaming out from the barracks in the neighbouring streets, singing and waving red flags. Paul's valet Demian was a reserve officer in the Preobrajensky Guards and he dashed out to his barracks around the corner to find out what was happening. He returned full of excitement: the Volynsky regiments had stormed into the Preobrajensky drill yard, killing an officer who tried to stop them and seizing weapons. From his study window, Paul could see, among the waves of soldiers, in their sand- and ash-coloured overcoats, the shoulder insignia of the Preobrajensky Guards. That mighty regiment, whose colours his grandfather had carried down the Champs Elysées in 1815, whose songs he knew by heart and in whose service the family had been raised to their place at their watching windows, was now breaking to pieces in front of his eyes. He watched them streaming past, half listening as former Cabinet colleagues phoned in with confident predictions that the disturbances would be put down. By the end of the afternoon, they were phoning in search of places to hide. He himself did not hide. He stayed where he was, watching the flood tide of revolution surging past his window.

The other Petrograd, the frozen people whom the Ignatieffs used to see from their car windows trudging homewards to their tenements, were coming towards them at last, scrambling across the Neva ice shouting, 'Bread! Bread!' and singing the Marseillaise. They carried blocks of ice in their hands, bolts, nuts and spanners, here a pistol, there an iron bar. As they scrambled up the embankment at dusk, the unthinkable thing finally happened: the Cossacks sheathed their sabres and let them pass. They surged on down the Liteiny Prospekt and met the advancing tide of leaderless soldiers. In the winter darkness, workers and soldiers together poured down Fourstatskaya street and the other streets that led to the Duma, bayonets bobbing and strips of red banner dancing over the heads. The Ignatieff family gazed out at them too astonished to be afraid.

Suddenly there were flag-decked barricades everywhere manned by soldiers and women muffled to the eyes. Suddenly there was shop glass and blood mixed with snow on the street corners; suddenly the old bearded policeman on the street corner who doffed his cap and wished them good health had vanished. In the forecourts of the Duma at the end of Fourstatskaya street, soldiers were milling around in their thousands; inside the corridors were piled with heaps of guns, sacks of barley and flour, the carcass of a pig, the corpse of a soldier with a bullet hole in his temple. Soldiers, students and workers were shouting, 'Where is the new power? Where is the new government?'

At an upstairs window in the house on Fourstatskaya street, Natasha parted the curtains with disdain. The scene below was 'atrocious, ignoble, shameful, never to be forgotten'. Who were these disreputable women, these animal-like men? The boys must not watch. It was not a show, not a theatre.

The lace curtains were pulled shut, the lights were turned off, the nurses and tutors were despatched to keep the boys back from the windows. But against orders, they crept along the darkened halls and, standing in the shadows, they watched the street below. All evening the muddy torrent of soldiers in uniform with red scraps of linen on their bayonets, students in green and light blue caps, workers in blue-visored hats, women in scarves and heavy

coats, poured by, making for the Duma. That first night of the
revolution the boys sat up in their bedrooms at the top of the
house and watched the courthouse burning two blocks away. Ash
tumbled through the night sky, settling on the pavements, stain-
ing and smudging the snow. In the livid panes of the upper-storey
windows opposite, they could see the reflected glow from the
courthouse pyre and a black plume of smoke vanishing upwards
into the dark.

In the days that followed there were excited phone calls from
the provisional government offering Paul the governorship of
Finland and other unspecified advancement in the new regime.
He refused everything except the presidency of the Russian Red
Cross. The provisional government sent a commission of inquiry
to interview him and told him his work at the ministry had been
an island of reform in a sea of reaction. The new Minister of
Education paid him a call and told him that when he had come to
the department to make the revolution, he found it had already
begun. When it became safe for bourgeois to be seen in the
streets, friends came to see him and talked hopefully about
piloting the bark of constitutional democracy across the seas of a
workers' and soldiers' uprising. He would have none of it. His
despair gave him a lucidity which saved him from the Micawber-
ish self-deceptions of his liberal friends. It was all finished, he
would mutter again and again, biting his lips, running his hands
distractedly through his hair.

I have my grandfather's diary for the year 1917. It is a
pocket-sized leather-bound volume with all the printed information a gentleman of Petrograd would want to know: the Orthodox
saints' days, the cycles of the moon and the Neva tides, the train
timetables to Moscow, Paris and Berlin, and the four-digit
telephone numbers of restaurants, hotels, ministries and Court
departments. On a few days in late February, Paul has noted
down his appointments; in early March there is a rather agitated
calculation of family finance scribbled in faint purple pencil.
After that, the fine cream pages of the diary are completely blank.

The depression that had descended upon him following his dismissal by the Tsar now turned into a complete nervous collapse, accompanied by a recurrence of violent asthmatic attacks and pains in the liver and chest. It was as if the symptoms of a neurosis suppressed but not confronted in Charcot's sanitorium twenty years before now chose the moment of the revolution to step out of the shadows of his life.

The revolution also accelerated a reversal in relations between Paul and Natasha. She had been first in her mother's shadow, then in Paul's. Now she came into her own. As Paul wasted away in the bedroom upstairs, it was Natasha who held the family together and protected him from the soldiers' and workers' deputations which began banging on the gates. She would let them in and have a maid serve them cucumber sandwiches. Most were just hungry and cold and they departed quite tamed. Natasha could not protect him from other deputations. Workers from Paul's cotton and glass factories arrived and stood in the hallway, their caps doffed, warming themselves against the radiators, politely listening to her when she said the master was ill but refusing to go away until she showed them up to the darkened bedroom where he lay in bed, white and drawn. He was helpless, unable to refuse them anything, but their demands were modest and they soon filed out, wishing him a long life.

Soon the revolution was less polite. In late March, a detachment of soldiers came to requisition the cars. They pounded on the gates while Basil the chauffeur struggled under the hood of the Mercedes to remove the distributor cap. When the soldiers found it was immobilized, they seized the Renault instead. The older boys were watching from the downstairs schoolroom window as one soldier took a red handkerchief out of his pocket, blew his nose, and then stuck the handkerchief on the bayonet out of the car window as it careened down the driveway. Demian managed to retrieve the Renault, abandoned and much the worse for wear, a few weeks later.

Throughout the revolution, Natasha was protected by her

certainties: the provisional government were contemptible weaklings; the women who demanded bread in the demonstrations were deluded, for shortages were imagined not real; the courageous police had been betrayed by officers who were half-witted and paralysed with indecision; the revolution was a crime and a blunder. What she watched from the window made her blind with anger. Years later, she wrote: 'Till my death day will I have the same firm belief that it was only slovenly weakness and thorough absence of knowledge of the nature of Russian crowds that let go this first disorder. If only a strong man knowing the Russian nature had arisen with a nice stick or our wonderful Empress Catherine the Great had come to life (I always venerated her ever so much more than Peter the Great as he copied all just like the monkey copying the master and by that destroyed much of the genuine Russian). Our Catherine loving and understanding our country but with a stick would put back all in order at the first, not when things went dragging along from day to day getting worse from total absence of energy and authority.'

When she talked like that Paul would always say half soothingly, half impatiently, 'Natasha, calm yourself, calm yourself!' He thought the truth was more complicated than her simple anger would allow. He had been in the very heart of the regime, he had seen the rottenness face to face; his disillusion was deeper than hers, and where she felt an anger that roused her to defence of her brood, he felt a despair that sapped him of the will to fight.

As for the children, the revolution was a wild street carnival they could not wait to get outside to see. The oldest boys were soon out in the street looking at the ruins of the courthouse and listening to the speeches on the steps of the Duma where a leaderless army had gathered to find leadership and absolution for its crimes. There was still a place for bourgeois boys like them at the fringes of a revolutionary crowd. Alec was eleven and was pissing against a wall near the Duma when a boy his age shouted, '*Bourgeois*, what are you doing?' and came towards him threateningly. An older worker shouted back, 'Leave him alone, he's a kid like you.' The boys mingled at the edge of the crowds listening to the slogans, each contradicting the other, which echoed above the din in the forecourt of the Duma:

'Fight Imperialist Germany!'

'Workers have not overthrown the Tsar to die for Capitalist Exploiters!'

'Secure the achievements of the Great Bloodless Revolution!'

'Down with the Imperialist War!'

Some speakers wanted to send the soldiers home to their villages and others wanted to send them back to the front. The soldiers shifted from speaker to speaker muttering, 'True! True!' now to one side, now to the other. The revolution debated its future, veering now this way, now that.

In the household on Fourstatskaya, the servants began to take sides. Demian, Koulakoff and Roman were active supporters of the revolution and while they continued at their posts there was a new edge in their relations with their masters. When Demian wanted a new suit, he pointed to one in Paul's cupboard and observed that it was worn out and needed replacement; he would then appear on his half day wearing it in the street. Koulakoff, the mild and inoffensive Cossack, acquired some backbone. When Monsieur Darier, the French tutor, observed that the bread was not a dirty grey colour in the house where his wife was governess, Koulakoff thumped another roll down on his side plate and told him what he could do with it if he didn't like it. Yet the same Koulakoff continued to wake the boys every morning, and supervise their washing and dressing; the stoveman kept piling the logs into the furnace; the serving girls kept bringing the dishes to the tables; and the milk churns from the Wassiltchikoff estate at Vybiti continued to arrive at the railway station and were picked up every morning by Basil the chauffeur. Even the bread eventually regained its old accustomed whiteness. There must have been moments in March and April when it was possible to believe the world outside would soon resume the measured order which had not skipped a beat inside the house on Fourstatskaya street.

But April turned to May and June. Lenin entered the city and began piloting the Bolsheviks towards the revolution of October.

Through the spring of 1917, Paul's condition worsened, and on 7 May a telegram arrived from Kroupodernitsa announcing the death of his mother. Father Nicholas was hastily summoned and Paul sang the *pannihida* in a broken voice. Natasha and the boys left him alone in his bedroom still clutching the telegram and hurried to the Church of Christ Walking Upon the Waters, where they lit candles and prayed for the repose of their grandmother's soul. A few weeks later Natasha moved Paul to a rented *dacha* in Tsarskoe Selo in the hope that the country air and distance from the downward vortex of the revolution in Petrograd would do him good. But he continued to lie in bed gazing at his inner wreckage.

On the front lines the disintegration of the army gathered momentum. In the Petrograd of May and June, crises and resignations followed each other at the heart of the provisional government; Lenin moved from house to house to avoid arrest. He spent several nights at the headquarters of the Central Trade Union, twelve houses away from the family home on Fourstatskaya. One of the boys is convinced that he saw him in the street or heard him speak from a platform. It is more likely that newsreels viewed in exile have seeped into his memory.

The family were safely out of the way in Tsarskoe Selo on the night of 3 and 4 July when Fourstatskaya again filled with a torrent of armed soldiers from the Bolshevik First Machine Gun Regiment and metal workers from the Putilov factories and sailors from Kronstadt marching on the Duma. By evening troops loyal to the government had regained control of the city and put down the insurrection. For the moment the provisional government held together, but it was clear to Paul and Natasha that the situation in Petrograd was slipping out of control. Once late at night, listening outside his father's bedroom door, one of the boys heard his father whisper to Uncle Boria Wassiltchikoff, 'I must get them out of here!' But when the children were assembled and told they were leaving for Kislovodsk, a spa town in the Caucasus mountains, five days by train to the south, the reason given was that their father needed to take a cure for his liver. Yet whatever she told her children, whatever she told herself, Natasha went to the bank and scooped up some of her jewellery from the safe-deposit box; she packed the volumes of her ancestor Karamzin's history of Russia and her photo albums of Doughino into the trunk she had bought in Nice for her trousseau.

The family was at the station two hours early, Paul looking gaunt and haggard, Natasha wandering around certain she had forgotten something and making jokes about her family's comic-opera migrations. Koulakoff ran around the platform like a sheepdog with his whiskers flying, piling cases into the compartments. It was an expedition on a grand scale: nannies, tutors, cooks, ladies' maids, seventeen people in all counting the boys and their mother and father. The first bell sounded, then the second. Last-minute checks of hand luggage were made. The family stood at the open windows and looked down at the platform: a mournful Demian left with the keys of the house on Fourstatskaya, Father Nicholas, the family priest, and a cluster of colleagues from the Ministry of Education who had come to say goodbye to their chief. The third bell sounded and the Caucasian express began to move out. Through the crowd burst an old man – a singer of folk tales who used to sing for the family – waving a birch stick which he passed up to Paul. On it there was a note saying, 'Be of good spirits and be sure of the results of your labour, as it has grown from a deep root.' It was dusk, the train glided away, and they waved their last farewells. As the train gathered speed, they stared out at the fields in the summer light. The land itself seemed to comfort them with the message that Petrograd and the revolution were not Russia: in the Ukraine the harvesters were out in the golden fields bringing in an abundant crop; the white convents of Orloff shone still in the summer evening and the country lanes were speckled with light through the poplars. They passed through Orel, Kharkov, Rostov, five

When my great-grandfather, N.P. Ignatieff, signed the Treaty of Peking in 1861, the Russian popular press celebrated his exploits.

Count and Countess Nicholas Ignatieff, Kroupodernitsa, *c.* 1900.

Natasha's father and mother, Prince and
Princess Mestchersky, 1890s.

Paul Ignatieff and his mother, Constantinople, 1872.

Doughino, the Mestchersky family estate, 1880s.

Doughino, interior, 1890s.

Kroupodernitsa, the Ignatieff family estate in the Ukraine, *c.* 1900.

Paul Ignatieff (1870–1945), my grandfather, in his twenties.

The Ignatieff family on holiday at Misdroy on the Baltic, with Peggy Meadowcroft, Tonia and a nursemaid, 1912.

A page from Peggy Meadowcroft's photograph album
of Kroupodernitsa, *c.* 1915.

The Rudnitsky family on the Ignatieff estate, Kroupodernitsa, 1915.

Paul Ignatieff with a file of convalescent soldiers, Kroupodernitsa, 1915.

Natasha Ignatieff in 1913.

The five-year-old George Ignatieff in Cossack costume, 1918.

Peggy Meadowcroft and the
Ignatieff boys, Putney, 1920.
From left to right: George (seated),
Nicholas, Alec, Dima and Lionel.

Natasha Ignatieff, 1920s.

Paul Ignatieff and farm-hands, Sussex, 1920s.

My father, first on the left, Kootenay Lake, Canada,
railroad gang, 1929.

Paul and Natasha Ignatieff, Upper Melbourne,
Quebec, 1944.

Michael Ignatieff and teachers, Kroupodernitsa, 1993.

Kroupodernitsa Church, 1993.

Priest's wife and family on the church steps, Kroupodernitsa, 1993.

My great-grandfather's grave,
Kroupodernitsa, 1993.

days on the train. The little ones – George and Lionel – leaned out of the windows at every station, imitating the singsong of the vendors who wandered up and down beneath the train windows selling apples and pretzels and a bread called *bubliki*. Enveloped in the calm of the countryside which passed their windows, it never occurred to the family to think they had left Petrograd for the last time.

SEVEN

THE CAUCASUS

———

The little spa town of Kislovodsk nestled in the foothills of the south Caucasus between the Caspian and Black seas. It had a Lilliputian railway station painted blue and white, a rotund concert hall and a scattering of rest-homes, villas and hotels clustered around the Narzan mineral springs, famous throughout Russia for their restorative effect on tired livers and digestions. The family rented a modest one-storey villa in the hills at the edge of town. There was a separate building for the servants and a large orchard of apple and plum trees. At first the summer of 1917 felt like all the other summers. The days in the Caucasus were hot and dry, the nights fragrant and cool. The boys played in the garden or went for hikes with Peggy in the hills. In her photograph album there are several pictures of the three oldest boys in Cossack caps eating sandwiches while perched on rocks in a steep canyon at the edge of town. But back at the villa, Paul sat slumped in a deck chair on the veranda locked in his depression. Once or twice a day he took a cab into town to sip the mineral waters. They had little effect.

The summer of 1917 was not like other summers. Kislovodsk was feverish, aglow like a tubercular patient. Oil barons from the Russian oil fields at Baku 200 miles to the southeast raced through the poplar-lined boulevards in their carriages, their drunken Caucasian guards firing revolvers in the air. The Grand Hotel overflowed with wounded officers sipping the Narzan waters and taking electrotherapy from society doctors. Up and down the trellis-covered walkways of the Vinogradnaya Alleya, the main promenade of the town, the strolling officers and their ladies pretended they were on holiday, not in flight. The arcades of the Narzan gallery, where Paul came to take the waters, were filled with Caucasian silver merchants and Armenian rug dealers and their wares. In the restaurants and outdoor cafés, waiters struggled to keep up with the custom; men in monocles and slicked-back hair snapped their fingers for service, ladies beckoned irately with their fans. On Fridays, the covered food market was full of Petrograd cooks and Moscow maids bargaining with Caucasian mountain people over melons and vegetables, tethered sheep and trussed chickens. Polite society kept up appearances, but on the quiet, it was starting to hawk its silver.

For the moment food was plentiful. The orchards and wheat fields of the south Caucasus were rich and bountiful. News of food shortages, pillaging gangs of deserters and clogged railways further north reached Kislovodsk as if from a distant planet. On the western front, the June offensive against the Austrians had ground to a halt and then turned into flight; the German army was closing in on Baku in the south and Riga in the north; yet in Kislovodsk none of the White officers seemed in a hurry to leave for the front.

Every day between eleven o'clock and noon, a Cossack band played martial airs at the bandstand in the main city park to an audience of officers and their ladies. One day in September, Dima and Nicholas, aged thirteen and fourteen, were there at the edge of the crowd when the music trailed off in a discord: someone had leaped onto the bandleader's podium and shoved the bandleader aside. From the back, the boys could see a slim figure in khaki standing on the conductor's podium and when they pushed closer they could hear a firm female voice. She shouted that she had just returned from the Riga front where the Germans had broken through and were sweeping everything before them. The soldiers had leaped from their trenches and had gunned down officers who tried to stop them. Then she turned on the crowd and shouted: 'Have you no shame! No patriotism! No comradely feeling! You loll about here while your fellow officers are being shot down by their own men, while your womenfolk have taken your place! Save Russia! Save those heroes and heroines! Form Battalions of Death!'

In the hush after she finished, a general next to the boys began to sob. Officers and their ladies surged toward her and swept her out of the park. She was fair-haired and frail with a harrowed look in her eyes. Men were saying, 'She is a Jeanne d'Arc! How she can speak! We must go! The first unit can be formed and leave in a couple of days!'

Next morning, the Kislovodsk papers referred to a regrettable incident at the bandstand, a hysterical outburst by a poor woman who needed rest and who should not have got mixed up in men's affairs. At noon that day, the orchestra played on and the officers and their ladies clapped as if nothing had happened.

For the oldest boy Nicholas, the scene at the bandstand laid bare the rotten core of the fruit. These generals who sobbed when she had finished, these Guardsmen whose uniform he had once dreamed he would wear, would not risk the crease in their tight leggings to defend their own country from the Germans. At the breakfast table, his father sipped his tea, sunk in his depression, saying nothing, adding to his son's disillusion by his silence. At night in secret, Nick began to fill his school notebook with earnest doggerel celebrating the dawn of the Revolution:

> In the East, the leaden night
> The orb of day repels
> Over Russia Freedom's light
> The night of gloom dispels.

In the autumn of 1917, Peggy Meadowcroft took a picture of young Nicholas sitting at his father's feet on the veranda steps, smiling and clutching his bare knees. Snow clings in wet clumps to the fruit trees in the foreground; in the background the hillside is white with snow. It is a bright day in late October. Paul is reclining in a deck chair, shrunken inside an overcoat, his face slack and puffy, the springs of energy in his body all run dry. He was slipping out of reach of his sons. If they asked him a question, it was minutes before he answered. He sat silently for hours, copies of his official reports to the Tsar on his knees.

In late October 1917, the local paper reported the storming of the Winter Palace, Kerensky's flight, the first decrees of the new Soviet power. In the last dismal hours, the only defenders of the frozen corridors of the palace had been the Women's Battalion, women like the one on the bandstand who had shouted through her tears in vain.

By the winter of 1918 Russia was plunged into civil war. White armies were in the field in Siberia, in the Crimea and in the north around Petrograd. But for the moment, the struggle was far away. For most of the autumn and winter the family went on as if the world beyond the green gates of their little house in Kislovodsk was still intact. The effects of the October Revolution did not reach the south Caucasus until a Soviet commissar, Kirov, proclaimed the advent of Soviet power from the balcony of the concert hall in the spring of 1918 and a Soviet of local workers replaced the old town council. But the lurid fears about what the Reds would do once they seized power did not materialize. The banks were nationalized but Paul managed to transfer his funds to a local cooperative society before his bank shut its doors for the last time. When the cooperatives were nationalized, he managed to withdraw his money and store it in an earthenware jar in the bathroom. Life kept on much as before. The boys began preparing for their gymnasium examinations with their tutors and managed to pass them in the spring. Paul kept up his routine of taking the waters though with no discernible effect on his health or his mood. Natasha ran the little troop of servants. The mountain people still brought their food to the Friday market.

By the early summer of 1918, General Denikin and General Wrangel's White armies were doing battle with Trotsky's Red armies in the north Caucasus, seventy miles away. Yet workers from Paul's factories near Moscow kept showing up in Kislo-vodsk, having traversed the zones of the civil war with letters from Paul's factory manager in their knapsacks and hard cash in their boots. Some of these messengers melted away into the civil war with their master's money, but most made it all the way. They would eat in the kitchen and sleep the night in the servants' quarters and then they would set off next day with their master's messages, to make their return crossing of a country cut in two by civil war.

One day in the spring of 1918, a disagreeable old soldier, Sergeant Yankevitch, with four St George's Crosses pinned to his tunic, arrived at the green gates with some frightened-looking Ukrainian serving girls in tow. Paul's sister, Mika, had despatch-ed them on a thousand-mile journey from Kroupodernitsa with potatoes and corn in their sacks and money in their boots. Grumbling all the way, Sergeant Yankevitch had carried out his mission and now wanted a good hot meal and a bed. He was the last of the messengers from the vanished life in the north, the last bearer of tidings from Kroupodernitsa and Countess Mika. She was now alone on the estate in the path of the German army marching into the Ukraine.

Paul pasted the money the old soldier had brought from Kroupodernitsa inside the upright piano in Peggy Meadowcroft's room. In the earthenware jar under the floorboards of the bathroom he hid Natasha's jewellery and his reports to the Tsar. Nothing had happened, but rumours told them searches and confiscations were about to start.

In early June 1918 they heard firing in the hills behind the town, then the grumbling of artillery and the screech of Red armoured trains on the railway lines. They learned that a party of marauding Cossack irregulars, under the command of a Tsarist colonel named Andrei Shkuro, were making raids on the Red defences at the edge of town. One morning, the family awoke to the chattering of a machine gun. Jumping up to his bedroom window, Nick saw a body lying in the roadway and soldiers in khaki advancing up the street. When it was safe to go out, Nick went into the garden where he found spent cartridges and a bloody bayonet.

Shkuro's cavalry rode into the city. Tsarist officers donned their old uniforms and women held out money and clothing to the Cossack horsemen. Here at last, everyone thought, was the advance guard of White victory. But Shkuro did not have the troops to hold the town. He swept in to rescue his wife from a Red hospital and swept out again, leaving the Whites to repent of their rejoicing. As the Reds moved back into the city, servants betrayed their masters, and neighbours betrayed each other to the Red authorities. In the mountains the Red cavalry burned Cossack villages.

Food began to go short. The mountain people stopped bringing their produce to market, and on Fridays Tonia and Koulakoff returned with their shopping bags empty. Paul roused himself from his torpor and set to work digging a vegetable garden in the back yard. But he was too weak to keep it up: handing the spade to Vaclav, the Czech gardener, he limped back to bed clutching his back, the colour draining from his face.

In August, Natasha decided Paul should take the mud-bath cures at Essentuki, another spa town nearby. Savage battles were being waged between the Red and White armies only forty miles away, yet at Essentuki Paul spent a reflective week up to his neck in mud in the company of two old generals wondering what had happened to the Tsar and his family. By then they were almost certainly dead. Paul returned to Kislovodsk, still no better, in time for Natasha's birthday. Five days later, on 30 August 1918, the head of the Petrograd secret police was assassinated, while in Moscow a Socialist Revolutionary assassin tried and failed to kill Lenin. In reprisal, terror was unleashed across Russia. The blacked-out cars filled with men in leather coats began making their nightly roundups.

They came for Paul on 6 September in the hours before dawn, pounding with their fists on the green gate, rattling the handles of the back veranda windows and hammering on the front door. Natasha shouted to Paul and the boys to stay in bed and rose to open the door. They swarmed past her through the house, twenty-five of them in all, led by a seaman from the Black Sea fleet named Tursky with a large diamond ring on his finger and drug-blurred eyes. Natasha felt herself shaking from head to foot, but she brought her voice under control and demanded to know what they wanted. The seaman asked her who lived in the house and he wanted to know whether her boys were of draftable age. She insisted that Nick, a tall fourteen-year-old, was really only twelve.

Then Paul appeared in the hallway, his greatcoat over his shoulders, gaunt and composed. The sailor handed him a search warrant signed by the Bolshevik Extraordinary Committee. They emptied his desk, took his ministerial briefcase and searched the high Dutch-tiled stoves. They found Natasha's housekeeping money, but when she pleaded that if they took it the family would be destitute, they returned it to her. One of the search party was a student wearing a cap from Moscow University. Paul remarked quietly, 'What a strange meeting, colleague,' and the student looked away. The leader of the search party then ordered his men to take Paul downtown for questioning. Paul kissed and blessed his children, and the men led him out into the street. Natasha dashed into the garden and called after them in the darkness, 'When will I see him again?' As they loaded him into an automobile, she heard someone shout back, 'Tomorrow morning early at the station.'

The car had only proceeded a short distance down the street when it stopped and the men went into another house to make a search. Paul sat in the car between two guards listening to the shouts and screams and banging of doors as the search party went about its work. After Paul had waited an hour outside, a soldier rode up to the car and ordered him to get out. Covered by a young soldier from behind, Paul walked the mile and a half down to the railway station through the silent streets. After half an hour, the soldier let Paul stop and rest. Sitting beside him on the curb, the soldier said he had been a student at the Technical Academy in Petrograd and had joined the Red Army because he had nothing to eat. Then he added in a whisper, 'This number will not go through.'

When Paul reached the Kislovodsk railway station, the local trade-union guards lifted him up gently into the freight car. When the Red guards taking the roll got to his name, the sergeant muttered that there must be some mistake. He had been a student in the local primary school: he remembered the teacher had once asked the class to stand and sing a song in praise of Count Paul Ignatieff. Paul clung to these hopeful signs even when he heard shooting outside the railway car at dawn, and saw a Red soldier sliding his revolver back in his pocket and barking an order to bury bodies in the ditch behind the car.

At first light, Natasha was running along the tracks by the station. She found Paul at last lying with a few other prisoners huddled in his overcoat in a freight car that stank of motor oil. Natasha bullied the man standing guard until he allowed her to approach to within arm's length of her husband. Paul looked weak and exhausted. They only had time for a few words before the guard ordered her away.

Natasha returned with her son Dima that afternoon, carrying Paul's medicine for his angina, a syringe, some bandages and yoghurt in glass jars. The sentry rummaged through the bandages, driving Natasha into a passion of rage. Screaming that his filthy hands had contaminated everything, she seized the yoghurt from Dima's hands and hurled it into the ditch. Paul watched her from the open door of the freight car. He said, 'Dearest, calm yourself, calm yourself.' Natasha returned to the railway siding at nightfall, but the car had been shunted some distance away and she wandered across the tracks looking for it in vain. Exhausted and desperate, she returned home again and informed the family that she was going to Bolshevik headquarters to protest at her husband's incarceration. The family pleaded with her to stay where she was: it was curfew, she risked being shot. A family friend named Professor Nechaev – who was collaborating with the Bolshevik Soviet in the running of the city's schools – had assembled a delegation to plead for Paul's life before the town Soviet. Natasha refused to listen, said good night to her children and took a cab down to Bolshevik headquarters in the Grand Hotel.

Through the long hours of that evening, she waited alone in the lobby for members of the Bolshevik committee to appear. Around midnight, a commissar named Atarbekov, a stout bull-faced man in a Cossack uniform with a red armband, passed through the lobby on his way to bed. She leaped up and demanded to know what he had done with her husband. He waved her away: he had just finished a heavy dinner and needed to sleep. Next there appeared the drugged sailor Tursky, who had been leader of the search party that had arrested Paul. He shouted that she risked being shot for being out after curfew, and Natasha replied that if she didn't find out what had happened to her husband, she didn't care if they did shoot her. Tursky then seemed to relent. He hinted that he might be able to do something next day. The former mayor of the town was in the lobby and appealed to Tursky to let her go home. One of Tursky's bodyguard accompanied her home, drunkenly recounting his 'work for the great bloodless revolution'.

Natasha heard that the prisoners were being taken by train to the Bolshevik headquarters in the south Caucasus at Piatigorsk, a spa town about twelve miles away. The next morning she secured a pass from her friend Professor Nechaev to go to Piatigorsk, authorized as a schoolteacher sent to buy sheet music for the schools. After another fruitless exchange of insults with the Bolsheviks at the Grand Hotel, she walked to the station, where friends and acquaintances clustered around whispering that all the prisoners were being brought to the station to be liberated. Just then she saw her husband being led from a railway car. Accosting Tursky, who was strutting along the platform with his guard at his side, she asked him when her husband would be liberated. 'He won't be liberated,' Tursky said with a smile.

She screamed at him, 'How dare you cheat me! You promised to let him go free.'

'I promised nothing.'

'Then I will accompany him.'

'You do not have a pass.'

'Yes I do!' she shouted. Reaching into her bag she grabbed a piece of paper and waved it in his face. He took it, examined it and returned it to her with a smile. She snatched it back. It was a shopping list. Aghast, she dug into her bag, found the real permit and handed it to him.

Tursky watched this comedy impassively. 'You won't go,' he said and turned his back on her.

At this moment, the doors of the station opened and the prisoners under guard were led to the train. Paul was among them; there were two Tsarist provincial governors she recognized and a party of Socialist Revolutionary opponents of the Bolsheviks who were carrying their bedding and singing revolutionary songs. Before Natasha and Paul could exchange a word the train moved out of the station towards Piatigorsk, which she knew had become a killing ground for White hostages. She felt like a stone dropped into a well.

Women on the platform comforted her, told her to be quiet, not to make a fuss. They told her to go home to her children. She did not go home to her children. All that day she sat in the lobby of the Grand Hotel, stunned and listless – half listening, half watching as the waiters passed to and fro in the lobby, as the Soviet committees argued behind the closed doors of the tea rooms and palm courts. Alone in her black dress and shawl, seated hour after hour of that long day, unnoticed by passers-by, she wondered in the unwounded part of herself how she would keep her sons alive now. She watched the September sun go down, distantly heard the shouts and clump of army boots in the marble hallway. Darkness roused her. She found a waiting cab and told the driver to take her home.

Her boys were all sitting in darkness: the electricity had been cut. In the silence and the darkness they sat together, stunned and motionless. To them, disaster had been a card always dealt to others. Everything their life had meant to that moment repeated the same reassuring message: you are immune. It will happen to others, but it will not happen to you. Now it was happening to them.

In the train to Piatigorsk, Paul was packed into the carriages with the Socialist Revolutionaries. As the blacked-out train crawled its way along the track, shunting around the edge of gunfire at the front, he sat muffled in his coat listening to the Socialist Revolutionaries sing the anthem 'We fell victims to the fatal struggle', which he had heard as a governor from his office window and which he now heard as a fellow prisoner of the new power. He thought he was about to die. The Socialist Revolutionaries thought he was about to die too. But they were sure that the Bolsheviks would spare them as fellow revolutionaries. At Piatigorsk station, the platform was filled with Red Army soldiers who pushed towards the hostages threateningly. The Ukrainian trade-union guards surrounded Paul and their leader shouted, 'The first one who moves towards us will be a dead man.' An old soldier from the Ukraine led him along the platform to a horse-drawn trolley. By this time Paul was scarcely able to walk. He leaned heavily on the soldier's arm. In the trolley that drew them along to the town prison, the old soldier, whispering, asked whether there was anything he could do to help. Paul just had time to reply: 'Tell the schools.'

Paul and the other prisoners from Kislovodsk were taken to a room at the entrance to the prison. Mr Gueh, chairman of the Bolshevik committee in Piatigorsk, a suave little man with bright intelligent eyes and a goatee, entered and asked in perfect French whether he could speak to Count Ignatieff. 'Citizen Ignatieff, you mean,' said Paul in Russian. Gueh seemed amused; the phone rang and Gueh went to answer it. Paul could hear a lady's voice inviting Gueh to tea and Gueh replying that he would be delighted to accept. Gueh excused himself and went back to the meeting to consider his prisoners' fates.

After a wash at the prison pump in the courtyard, Paul was led into a large room: provincial governors, Jewish merchants, judges, army officers, Serbs, Poles, Tsarists and Socialist Revolutionaries all lay against the whitewashed walls waiting. There was an old armchair in the middle of the room. The prisoners led him to it and sat him gently down.

Just before eight o'clock, the prisoners heard footsteps in the passage. The door opened and Atarbekov, the bull-like Bolshevik whom Natasha had accosted in the hotel lobby in Kislovodsk the night before, appeared with the prison superintendent and a guard. They pointed at citizen Ignatieff.

'You are free. Leave the prison immediately.'

Paul said he would not leave without the others. Atarbekov pointed to two Tsarist former governors whom Paul had befriended in the railway car and said, 'Take them quickly.'

'You will give us a certificate that we are free?' Paul asked.

'I have no office here and no stamp so I cannot give you any documents,' Atarbekov replied.

'Then I shall not leave the prison. The town is under martial law, and I prefer to be shot in the regular way to being shot like a dog in a dark street corner.'

One of the prisoners was tugging at Paul's elbow urging him to make a run for it. But Paul was adamant. Why, he insisted, had he been arrested at all and why now was he being told to leave?

Atarbekov replied gruffly, 'We did not know that you had been useful to national education.' One of the prison guards chimed in, 'You may not know, but we knew.' In heavily accented Russian the guard explained that he had been a pupil at a textile vocational school in Lodz in Poland, funded and encouraged while Paul was minister. Paul said he would be willing to leave the prison with this man. He then demanded that Atarbekov phone the Kislovodsk Soviet to tell them he was free and to inform his family.

The Ukrainian trade unionists had done as Paul had told them: they had gone to the schools and had happened on a teachers' council in session. A local teacher named Oudariuk who had joined the Bolsheviks and helped them in map-reading in the Caucasus told the trade unionists to spread the word about the arrest of Count Ignatieff among the local schools. Soon teachers and students from all over town were gathered under the windows of the Bolshevik headquarters, standing silently in the autumn twilight. The Bolshevik teacher went into the meeting and demanded Paul's liberation. When Gueh began to protest, the teacher gestured to the crowd below and told him they would liberate the prisoner by force. The Bolshevik hold on the town was uncertain: the Whites were in the hills, and all available detachments were at the front. An uprising of the citizens of the town had just been suppressed. The only guards at Gueh's disposal were members of the Polish Legion and they had refused to do anything other than guard duty: they would not intervene against the crowd. Gueh's hand was forced. He ordered the immediate liberation of the prisoner. Paul owed his life to the capricious fortune of civil war, to some Ukrainian trade unionists and to a young Bolshevik geography teacher he had never met.

Back at the villa in Kislovodsk, the boys were lying awake in the darkness when the phone rang in the passageway. They heard their mother's excited voice, and before they could clamber out of bed, she rushed into their room: 'He is free! He is free!' The thing seemed impossible – no one could sleep that night wondering whether to believe the news.

That night, Paul lay on the prison floor, listening to the tubercular coughing of one of the prisoners, wondering whether to believe that he would be free next day. Next morning, Atarbekov did produce a document certifying that the Ignatieffs could continue to live unmolested in Kislovodsk. With the prisoners whose release he had demanded as a condition of his own, Paul was freed and took the train back to Kislovodsk. In the late afternoon, after forty-eight hours of imprisonment, Paul returned to the family villa. Peggy Meadowcroft gave him a cigarette 'to stiffen him up': it was the first he had ever smoked. His sons can still see their father, gaunt and haggard, standing in his greatcoat smoking that cigarette in the passageway of the darkened villa on Bayazetskaya street. It was – Dima says – the most important moment of his life.

Next day when Natasha was shopping in the Vinogradnaya Alleya she saw a man reading a newspaper with an expression of horror on his face. She went up and he pointed at a column of 140 names, the list of the White prisoners executed by the Red firing squad on the slopes of Mount Mashuk on the outskirts of Piatigorsk. Among the names were those of the two generals with whom Paul had shared the mud baths of Essentuki two weeks before; the Socialist Revolutionaries who had sung 'We fell victims to the fatal struggle' in Paul's railway car; and nearly all of the frightened men who had offered him the only chair in the prison cell in Piatigorsk. Tsarists and Socialist Revolutionaries were tossed into the same shallow grave. Half way down the newspaper column, Natasha found Paul's name.

Two days after his release Kislovodsk changed hands. Colonel Shkuro's Cossacks rode back in from the hills. Nick was chopping wood in the front yard when an evil-looking Cossack whose uniform hung on him in tatters banged on the gate and asked if they had any shirts or trousers to spare. Nick did have a pair of new breeches made from khaki cloth sent from the family factories. He gave these to the Cossack, before realizing that he had left himself with only the knee pants he was wearing. While the Cossack stood at the gate spreading the breeches over his tattered legs, Nick asked him what kind of government they would set up when the White armies had taken Moscow. Would they restore the monarchy?

'Monarchy, nothing! When we are through with these Bolshevik devils, we'll cut all the aristocrats' throats, the bloodsuckers!' He took the breeches and rode off.

Several weeks later, the oldest boys were out walking with Peggy Meadowcroft in the parched hills at the edge of town when they came across a party of Caucasian mountaineers who told them that the Reds were about to return to Kislovodsk. 'What will happen then,' the boys asked. The men with their grizzled faces and shaggy hats smiled and drew a line across their throats with the point of their daggers. When Peggy and the boys got home everyone was safe but there was already a Red battery on Coffin Mountain pounding the outskirts of town and a White battery replying to the fire, sending columns of earth shooting up from the mountain's flanks. In the afternoon, Nick clambered over the garden wall and stole away up the hillside to get a better look. He lay on the parched grass, feeling the last autumn heat in the earth, and watched the eddying line of a battle on the grasslands above the town, six miles away. White puffs of smoke rose from cannon mouths, bodies ran and fell and lay still. It was like a painting in a museum.

The clatter of machine guns close by drove him back over the garden wall to the safety of the villa. Shrapnel was bursting over the roads near the house. The Reds were bombarding the railway station. Soon Hludovskaya street, the road at the bottom of the garden, was clogged with fearful White families fleeing to the hills. Natasha's brother Peter was among them, leaving his family behind while he went to join Colonel Shkuro's White Cossack forces.

Paul was too ill to move, and besides he put no faith in Shkuro or any of the Whites. So all that afternoon the family watched from the window as the silent, desperate column tramped past their window and disappeared in a plume of dust into the distance. By dusk, the White Cossack cavalry were retreating up the road from the advancing Red forces. From the veranda the boys could see the crimson puffs of shrapnel bursting over the fleeing White civilians. Paul and Natasha and their children settled down to dinner in darkness, in a town awaiting invasion. After dark, they heard the rumble of a Red armoured train arriving at the railway station and from the town below there rose the faint sound of a band playing the *Internationale*.

The next months of Red occupation, from October 1918 to late January 1919, were a nightmare blur of searches, rumour, hunger and cold. Seventeen times armed parties ransacked the house searching for weapons, contraband, jewels, food and fuel. The family managed to hide some things in Peggy Meadowcroft's upright piano. She pinned a Union Jack to the door of her room and when they came to search she stood before the door and declared in Putney Russian that her room was British territory and they had no right to enter. Then she would sit down at the piano and pound out 'It's A Long Long Way To Tipperary' to keep up family morale. Everything else that was precious, the jewels, the last of the money and the reports to the Tsar, were safely hidden in the earthenware jar under the floorboards in the bathroom, but after the sixteenth search books, icons, silver and linen were gone. Every time it seemed as if it was over, they would return, lock everyone in their rooms and start all over again.

When they had taken everything else, the ragged and hungry men came a seventeenth time and tipped the contents of the children's drawers and cupboards onto bed sheets, knotted them up and carried them off. Natasha insisted that they at least leave shoes for the children. One of the searchers looked at her and said the citizeness did not understand: his own children had never had any shoes.

Bit by bit, the old sustaining order of cooks and ladies' maids, footmen and butlers melted away. Koulakoff the butler became too openly Bolshevik in his sympathies: he was dismissed. The cook, in Natasha's words, 'behaved ignobly' with Katia, the ladies' maid, and made her pregnant. The two of them were dismissed, though they continued to live in the town and Natasha continued to visit Katia to seek advice and help. When one of the tutors returned from a visit to the north of Russia and came back in Natasha's words 'a regular wild man of the forest, dirty, all covered with hair, altogether a physical and moral bolshevik', he too was sent packing. Soon only a handful of the servants who had made the journey from Petrograd remained.

George, the youngest boy, lived throughout the revolution like a bird under the wing of his nurse Mania. She had raised him from infancy, steadied him when he took his first steps in the dark garden of the villa in Tsarskoe Selo, spread the white linen sheets in the train compartment to keep him from the soot of the journey south from Petrograd, dressed him up in a Cossack's uniform to be photographed and sat with him through the night they took his father away. She was a slight, brown-eyed Siberian peasant girl of implacable devotion who came to believe that George was really her baby.

One winter night in late 1918, while George was asleep, Mania was dismissed and told to leave the villa. George, then just six years old, awoke the next morning and instead of Mania found the tutor reaching down to pull him out of bed. George held on for dear life to his bedpost and when yanked clear in the struggle he hit his head and passed out. He woke up in Peggy Meadowcroft's room, panic-stricken and sore, listening to her say that he was now a big boy and would have to get along without his Mania.

Pitched out of the nursery world, he now began to be aware of the world beyond the villa gates. It was only after Mania's departure that his memory received its first imprint of horror. From the windows of the villa, he saw a man being dragged screaming along the dusty street just outside the green gates, his legs tied to the back of a horse, his captor riding along not even bothering to look back.

That autumn of 1918 the boys first became aware of how much the times had changed their mother. She was no longer the frail, vague, comical and retiring figure of their childhood in Petrograd. Hardship had weathered her. During their father's arrest, she had been like a tigress, enraged, tenacious and unafraid. Now that most of the servants had gone, she took over the housekeeping. She had never so much as boiled water in her life before. Now they watched her leave the house in the morning dressed in a shabby black overcoat, with her hair in a peasant woman's shawl, to queue at the baker's for crumbling loaves made out of corn, potato flour and bran. One of the boys went with her when she travelled out into the villages to bargain for mutton, cooking fat and honey. She had become sharp and shrewd and resilient. And she never railed at fate.

She had nothing but scorn for relatives in town who played cards with the Red commissars and who served tea and sandwiches for the search parties who came to ransack their houses. Natasha's rage, her sense of violation, made her fearless. When the search parties tried to take the children's clothes, she shouted at them; when they took her husband's family seal and Karamzin's history of Russia, she stormed down to Bolshevik headquarters to demand their return. When the commissars threatened her with imprisonment if she didn't clear off, she dared them to try. She astonished herself and her children. They knew she was terrified of mice and thunderstorms, but she was not afraid of anything else.

When the winter came in November 1918, the boys helped Vaclav the gardener chop down the poplars in the garden for fuel. They fed the green logs into the stoves to keep warm. Smoke filled the house and ice formed inside the cracks in the walls. The boys wore all their clothes at once, old army boots and potato sacking on their feet. The loaves in the market grew smaller, mouldier, more evil-smelling. The money was gone and they lived on fruit from the villa orchard, the mouldy bread and mutton broth. Vaclav could see the boys were going hungry. He went to his woodshed and pulled out his secret store and came to the Count and offered him a wad of Kerensky rubles. Paul accepted in tears.

The Whites settled into a siege of the spa towns and every day the windows rattled with the thump of artillery duels in the mountains. Two of the boys, Alec and Dima, began to write and edit a small newspaper which they sold to the neighbouring families. After a few weeks, when Alec wrote a lead story beginning, 'Last night firing was heard,' Dima said he would never make a journalist. What kind of story was that? There was firing every night.

Far away on the western front, the Great War came to an end. At first Paul and Natasha thought the armistice would free the Allies to increase their support to the Whites. They expected deliverance hourly, waiting like supplicants for the tender mercies of the Whites. But as Christmas came, Paul and Peggy Meadowcroft sat in the smoky darkness with candles trying to plot a route of escape southwards across the mountains into Persia. Christmas 1918 was funereal. They all gathered in the dining room for evening service. Their local priest, Father Naum, led them in prayer and Paul sang the responses in a weak, unsteady voice.

They were singing vespers again one wintry night in January 1919 when a neighbour burst in with news that General Wrangel's White Army had retaken the town. This time deliverance was sickening in its vengefulness. The Whites slaughtered men, women and children who were retreating in the rear of the Red Army on the snowy roads to Stavropol. They erected a gallows on Hludovskaya street, within sight of the villa, and executed Xenia Gueh, the wife of the French-speaking Bolshevik commissar of Piatigorsk, together with the White lover who had tried to help her escape when the Whites surrounded the National Hotel. On the day of the execution, Paul came into the boys' room and drew the shutters so they wouldn't look. They looked anyway and saw the hooded bodies turning in the wind with signs saying 'Traitor' around their necks.

Because Paul had survived the massacre of Piatigorsk, had refused to flee with Shkuro and had survived under the Red regime, the White authorities regarded the Ignatieffs with suspicion. The Whites arrested naive Professor Nechaev for cooperating with the Bolsheviks and when Paul went to the new White chief of secret police to demand Nechaev's release, the man threatened to have him arrested too. 'Just try,' was Paul's reply.

Princess Panin, the only female minister in the government that General Denikin had formed to rule the territory in the Caucasus under White control, came to Paul and offered him the Ministry of Agriculture in the government they felt sure would be established when Moscow fell to the Whites in the spring. Paul asked Princess Panin what the White policy towards the peasantry would be. She replied that the land seized from the landholders would be given back. 'It is impossible to tolerate such lawlessness and the triumph of the "property grabbers".' Paul replied coldly, 'So we accept from the revolution only what is pleasing to us?' He refused to have anything to do with the White administration.

As January turned to February, the hostility of the Whites and fears of the return of the Reds convinced Paul that he must get his family to safety. At first the Crimea seemed a possible port of escape but the White hold on Odessa began to slip. When British intelligence officers with Denikin's army arrived in Kislovodsk from the Black Sea port of Novorossisk, 100 miles to the northwest, Peggy Meadowcroft went back with them to Novorossisk to find a ship. She returned with news that there was a British cruiser and a supply ship in the harbour that might be able to take them on board.

First the family had to escape the clutches of the local Whites. A train coach put at the family's disposal by the Russian Red Cross was intercepted by the local White police, and a car sent by the Denikin government to take them to Novorossisk never arrived. By late January 1919, the Reds were in the hills outside the town, the railway lines were dynamited in many places. The whole country between the spa towns and the Black Sea was laid waste, and typhus and smallpox were raging. At this juncture their luck held. The wife of General Wrangel, who had come to Kislovodsk to convalesce from an attack of typhus, agreed to put the general's private railway coach at their disposal.

They left one cold February evening, all their possessions hastily packed in the faithful trousseau trunk, the jewels and money retrieved from the earthenware jar, the boys wrapped in all the clothing they had left. They said goodbye to Father Naum, to Koulakoff and Katia and Vaclav, who was clutching the money which Paul had managed to repay. Each knew they would never see the other again. The railway car was pitch black; the wind whistled in through broken windows, the trimmings and upholstery were ripped away, and the car was filled to bursting with other fleeing refugees. As the train gained speed, a haunting baritone voice started to sing in the darkness, and shadows took up the song until the whole darkened car was in full voice as it swept through the snowy night.

A journey which should have taken half a day took three days. The train crawled through a flat, blasted landscape dotted with frozen corpses, abandoned wagons and army horses rigid in the poses of death. At Mineralni Vodi station, which had been bright with the kerchiefs of peasant women and their full fruit baskets when they passed through before, the platform was crowded with starving, numb refugees who stared at the shocked white-faced Ignatieff boys in their warm carriage. There was a worse sight at the carriage window opposite. On the track next to theirs stood a railway flatcar loaded with snow-covered typhus corpses.

When they arrived in Novorossisk, the family rented rooms in a merchant's house overlooking the port and Peggy Meadowcroft set about establishing contact with the crew of the British cruiser, the *Grafton*, and an old British steamship, the *Huanchaco*, pressed into service as a troop transport. Both ships were in the harbour to bring supplies and assistance to the White forces. While they waited for their passage, the family saw still more White misrule. Nick watched from the windows of their rented rooms while Red prisoners, 'pale ghosts, walking skeletons, scarcely human', were driven down the street and White officers on horseback mounted the pavement and forced every passer-by to doff their hats to the imperial eagle. Paul would close the curtains with disgust. From Odessa came rumours, which soon proved to be true, that the retreating White command was towing Red soldiers out in barges into the middle of the Black Sea and drowning them. Caught between Reds and Whites the family became desperate to leave.

Out in Novorossisk harbour lay their salvation: HMS *Grafton* and the *Huanchaco*. Peggy Meadowcroft went down to the quay and put her charm to work on the ship's company. British officers came courting Peggy on the sofa, while the family hung back behind the closed doors of the cramped rented rooms. At night when there were rumours of incursions by bandits from the hills, the *Grafton* played its searchlights on their house to keep them safe. The boys went to sleep with the beams sending shivers of light through the shutters onto the ceiling. Salvation was as close as the source of the searchlight beam, but before the British could take them on board, the family needed exit visas from the Whites. January turned into February and February into March. The wind howled along the quays. Still no visas arrived. The Crimea fell and the Red armies closed in on Novorossisk. Panic-stricken refugees and disintegrating units of the White Army thronged the port. The clamour for places on the British boats grew intense. For several hundred pounds sterling Paul sold off half of his interest in his factories to four Moscow merchants who left rubbing their hands with glee at the bargain that misery had forced him to strike. This time, Paul's feeling of exhausted depression settled over Natasha.

Peggy Meadowcroft seized the initiative. She found a place on a filthy troop train leaving for Ekaterinadar, where the visas were issued. For twelve hours she fought off the attentions of the White soldiers on board the train and arrived in a fine fury at White headquarters. Astonished by this indefatigable English nanny hectoring them in Russian, the Whites capitulated. Triumphantly, she returned to Novorissisk with the necessary papers. Soon Mr Hough, one of the officers of the *Huanchaco*, had fallen in love with her. Privately he urged her to leave the family but she refused. She said she must get her boys into good schools in England. Mr Hough found the family a place on the ship.

One morning in May a truck arrived from the *Huanchaco* to cart away the sole remaining family trunk. Mr Hough arrived soon after to say they were about to weigh anchor: he found a Te Deum in progress, and the family in the sitting room saying the prayers offered on a great departure. He sat cap in hand in the anteroom until he could stand it no longer. He hissed in Peggy's ear that they must be going. A stretcher was brought for Paul – he was too weak to walk – and they all drove down to the quay and marched up the gangplank. At dusk the ship weighed anchor and the family stood by the taff rail and watched the last horizon of Russia vanish on the lip of the waves.

The *Huanchaco* steamed back and forth across the Black Sea for three weeks. They sailed to Batum, where the boys watched as Indian Sikhs of the British army in Turkey chivvied and smacked a load of mules up the gangplanks. Then they sailed to Constanza, a port in Rumania, where the mules were unloaded. The boys worked on their English with the sailors and the sailors gave them English nicknames that stuck to them for life: Jim, Nick, Alec, Lino and Georgy. The boys noticed that Peggy stopped calling their father and mother Count and Countess. For the first time they became Paul and Natasha. Their father didn't seem to mind but their mother stiffened whenever Peggy spoke.

From Constanza the ship made its way to Varna in Bulgaria. Bulgarians had fought on the German side against the Russian armies and for this reason Paul would not let the boys land, though they could see the sandy beach and the children playing, and Paul knew that there was a statue to his father, the father of modern Bulgaria, in the city square. When news leaked out that the son of Count Nicholas Ignatieff, liberator of Bulgaria from the Turkish yoke in 1877, was on board, the mayor arrived with a civic delegation to beg him to land. 'Are your bayonets dry?' Paul wanted to know. The mayor looked down at his shoes and pleaded that Bulgaria be forgiven. So they landed and the refugee and his family were able to gaze for the last time at his father, frozen at the height of his imperial glory, staring unseeing over the square.

As the *Huanchaco* neared Constantinople and entered the Bosphorus on the last morning of the voyage, the ship was boarded by British and French intelligence agents who asked Paul where he was born. He looked out of the window and said quietly, 'Constantinople.' They told him to be serious, and he said he was perfectly serious. There, just as he spoke, the ship passed below the gleaming white walls of the Russian ambassador's summer residence high on the bluffs of Byouk Dere. Standing there in the line with the other refugees Paul could look up and point to the second-storey window where he had been born.

EIGHT

SAVAGE LANDS AFAR

While the family waited on board the *Huanchaco* in Constantinople harbour, Paul made his way up the hill to the Russian embassy, hoping the embassy would issue him and his family with papers that would allow them to continue their journey to England. At the entrance, he found that the gatekeeper was the son of the one who had been there in his childhood. The gatekeeper said the embassy was now occupied by a bad lot, representatives of General Denikin's White government in southern Russia. 'If I were you,' the gatekeeper said, 'I wouldn't go in there. Go and get the consul general, a man of the old school, to have a talk with Denikin's people first.' So Paul went and found the consul general and they came back to the embassy. Paul sat in the big hall while the consul general argued with Denikin's representative in a room that had once been his father's study. The consul general soon came out, muttering furiously that Denikin's representative had refused to help, saying, 'I do not yet know if the presence of Ignatieff in Europe is desirable.'

Exhausted and despondent, Paul hurried back to the port to find the whole family dumped on the quay and the *Huanchaco* disappearing in the distance. Paul sat down on the trunk and despatched Natasha to find some rooms for the night. While she dashed from one seedy boarding house to another, Peggy and the boys wandered forlornly up and down the quay, which was thronged with Levantine traders and Turkish stevedores manhandling boxes, barrels and crates. The three weeks on board the *Huanchaco* had delayed the shock of exile. Now it hit them all with full force. Natasha returned, having been promised a room by a Frenchman she had met in the street. When they arrived at the boarding house, the Frenchwoman who ran the place took one look at the dusty family and shooed them away. They traipsed from one tatty hotel to another until they found rooms, as night fell, in a miserable and verminous boarding house run by a kindhearted Armenian woman whose face was bruised from her husband's beatings. They dined on greasy broth and locust beans from the carob trees outside the window and bedded down, all eight of them, in a pair of rooms. George slept in a chest of drawers. Thus they spent the first nights of exile.

When the Russian consul general found out where they were living, he took pity on them and moved them into his own apartment. Through contacts with the Russian provisional government in exile in Paris, Paul was soon able to force the Denikin representative to issue him with papers. The British still refused to admit the family, but Paul managed to secure a visa for France. But it took weeks before a ship could be found. When Paul tried to change his remaining rubles on the black market, his wallet was stolen and the family would have starved had it not been for a loan from a generous refugee friend. It was not until the end of June 1919 that the family managed to end its accursed stay in Constantinople. They boarded *La Flandre*, a passenger ship still filthy from its use as a troop ship, and sailed for France. They landed in Marseilles, made their way to the station and boarded a train for Paris jammed with demobilized French soldiers laughing and joking on their way home. In their midst sat the penniless Ignatieffs with Peggy Meadowcroft.

At the Gare de Lyon in Paris they were met by Paul's cousin, Colonel Alexis Ignatieff, who had been Russian military attaché in Paris during the war and whose father, Paul's uncle, was the governor of Tver province gunned down by an assassin in 1906. Alexis whisked them home to the fashionable apartment in St Cloud where he lived with his ballerina mistress and turned the boys loose on a real Russian feast. After a year of near starvation, the *koulibiaka, koulitch, blini* and *kissail* were like a promise of deliverance. Uncle Alyosha, as the boys called him, regaled them with stories of the time he quelled a mutiny among the Russian troops sent to join French forces on the Western Front in 1916. He told them about his meetings with Clemenceau, Joffre and Foch, all the great men of the war. It was several days before the family realized their cousin was the most hated man in the Russian émigré community. As Russian military attaché he had been entrusted with huge sums for the procurement of military supplies from French arms manufacturers. In November 1917, he transferred his allegiance to Lenin and helped procure munitions for the Red armies. Alyosha was only settling an old score. He believed his father had been gunned down not by Socialist Revolutionaries but by the Tsar's own secret police who wanted to eliminate his father for opposing the Tsar's concessions after the 1905 revolution. Alyosha felt free to betray a regime that had first betrayed him. Shunned by the entire émigré community and distrusted by the commissars who took over the Paris embassy, Uncle Alyosha must have been glad to see his cousin Paul, especially since Paul had his own reasons for distrusting the various White regimes in exile. Alyosha set the family up in a modest *pension* while they waited for visas to England.

Natasha decided she must go to cooking school to learn the rudiments of providing for her family. So she enrolled at Cordon Bleu, the only cooking school she had ever heard of, not bothering to ask how much the lessons cost. At her first lesson she learned how to cook a *risotto*, and at her second she learned how to make *marrons glacés*, glazed chestnuts. Those were the only cooking lessons she could afford, and so those two dishes became the dreary staple of family diet.

It would have been natural for the family to have remained in Paris. It was the capital of the Russian émigré community. The headquarters of the Russian Red Cross in exile, of which Paul was president, had been established there. French was Paul's second language. Yet he was determined to get to England. He knew that a Liverpool broker owed him money for a transaction involving cotton deliveries to Paul's factories near Moscow. If he could find the broker and get him to honour the debt, the family's destitution could be remedied. Paul also admired English education and both he and Peggy were determined to get the boys enrolled in a good school. Two years of civil war had done much more than interrupt their education; Paul feared that it had turned his oldest son, Nick, into a Bolshevik fellow traveller. A strict English education would turn them into proper English gentlemen and vaccinate them forever against wild politics. What Natasha thought of this plan, what she thought of Paul's increasing dependence on Peggy, she kept to herself.

In late July 1919, they arrived in London and went to stay with Peggy Meadowcroft's mother in her flat in a three-storey late-Victorian terrace house at 10A Oxford Road in Putney, a mile or so from Putney Bridge. Peggy moved in with her mother and gave her bedroom to Paul and Natasha while the boys were crammed in under the eaves in the attic. It must have been a cheerless summer for the boys, reconnoitring the streets of Putney, feeling hard looks directed at them from behind lace curtains, struggling to master a few English phrases for use in sweetshops and cafés. 10A Oxford Road was cramped and depressing, with a mean little English garden squeezed in between fences, where Peggy made them pose for her Brownie camera. In these pictures, the older boys are standing stiffly at attention in their new English suits, uncomfortable inside their enamel-hard Eton collars, their gangling arms held stiffly at their sides and their cuffs riding above their button boots. The younger ones are wearing sailor suits with knee pants and sport sailor caps with the names of Royal Navy warships on the hatbands. By then Peggy had taught them their first English song: 'Rule Britannia'.

The youngest boy, George, was six that lonely summer. Soon after their arrival. he remembered, the family went to a Russian

Orthodox church somewhere behind Victoria Station and stood for hours during an interminable Sunday service at which the Dowager Empress, the Tsar's mother, was present. It was hot and stuffy and soon George's head was swimming. Old ladies went round to the burning candles in front of the icons, deftly snuffing out the ones which burned down low, pinching life out between their fingers. The priest swung the censer, the incense rose in clouds around the altar, the choir droned on and George felt his legs give way beneath him. Someone picked him up and carried him outside. He came to in a superb car with mahogany fittings, grey cushions and leather upholstery. A chauffeur in livery was fanning his face with his cap. At first he thought that he was in heaven and then in Petrograd and that all the dreadful times in Kislovodsk and Constantinople had not really happened. He heard his mother say that he was still weak from the effects of malnutrition and so he knew he was in London after all. While his brothers looked through the windows, Natasha explained that he was in the Rolls-Royce of the Dowager Empress. She herself was still inside the church, standing as stiff and straight as she had stood earlier that summer on the afterdeck of HMS *Marlborough*, watching with a kerchief in her hands as the shores of the Crimea slipped from sight.

Later in that summer of 1919, George and his brothers stood in the crowds with their father while General Haig marched up Pall Mall past Buckingham Palace at the head of a triumphant Allied victory parade. There were French and Belgian contingents but no Russian one, despite the millions of lives lost on the Eastern Front. The Bolsheviks' separate peace with the Germans at Brest Litovsk in the winter of 1918 had seen to that. Old Russia was now a disgraced and forgotten ally and the new Soviet regime was fighting Allied contingents on various fronts of the civil war. In the braying crowd, in the blizzard of Union Jacks, the family felt alone and apart. 'Remember, Paul, Russia is a defeated nation,' the boys heard Peggy say. They were a defeated family and Peggy believed herself to be their saviour. She did not let them forget it. Paul had told her to turn the boys into English gentlemen and Peggy set about her task with a vengeance. In the tiny rooms of the flat in Oxford Road, the boys rose promptly at seven, had a stout English breakfast, a bowel movement promptly after breakfast on pain of punishment, and then hours of lessons. They were not to fraternize with boys in the street and games of any kind were forbidden. After dinner at six, the boys were supposed to practise their musical instruments until lights out at seven.

To cure George of the malnutrition that had caused him to faint in church, Dr Batteshaw, a paediatrician in Harley Street, prescribed a daily meal of fat bacon rashers. Peggy stood over him to make sure he ate every bite. 'What did Mr Batteshaw say?' she would bark whenever he stopped chewing. 'Fat, Peggy,' he would say, choking on tears and bacon. Lionel, two years older than George, went around with a look of permanent terror in his eyes from the punishment that Peggy administered when he missed a note on his violin. She would rap their knuckles with the ruler and make them write fifty times over, 'I am a naughty boy,' in their exercise books. Worse than her dark regime was the knowledge that their parents seemed to approve. At least Paul did: his instructions to Peggy were clear enough and Natasha kept silent, distracted by continuing anxiety about Paul's health and aware, as they all were, that destitution had made them utterly dependent on their nanny.

They were penniless when they arrived in England, but there was the matter of the Liverpool cotton broker who owed him something like £25,000 sterling for Egyptian cotton which Paul had paid for but which the war had prevented from being shipped to his factories. The money Paul had paid for the cotton had been deposited in an English bank. A month or so after their arrival, Paul saw a notice in *The Times* to the effect that Count Ignatieff should get in touch with the Midland Bank, where he would find information to his benefit. Paul had no papers, no proof of his identity, but as luck would have it, he ran into his Moscow lawyer on his way into the bank and together they managed to prove the money was his.

In the autumn and winter, Paul checked into a rest-home to recover his health and Natasha began touring the estate agents in search of a house. The older boys were sent to a school in East Grinstead to prepare for the entrance exams to St Paul's School. The topics for the exam essay were 'What Elephants Do in the Zoo', 'English Railway Termini' and 'Profiteering'. Dima – fourteen at the time – wrote his essay on the prophets Elijah and Moses, Ezekiel and Jeremiah. Despite humiliations like this and jeers from English boys that they were little Bolshies, the boys soon mastered English and in the spring they were accepted at St Paul's.

In the summer of 1920, the family moved to the farm Natasha had found between Hastings and Battle on the Sussex coast. There was a dairy herd, eighty acres of farmland, 170 acres of woodland, a farmhouse and on a hill overlooking the whole property a rambling Victorian brick house called Beauchamps. It had splendid arched doorways, stained-glass windows on the stairway, high ceilings in the dining room and sitting room and a warren of bedrooms under the eaves where the boys slept. From the high-gabled rooftop, where the boys quickly learned to scramble when their mother wasn't watching, they could look out over the trees at the English Channel. Natasha called it Beechums, and Paul called it Kroupodernitsa. He had recovered his health by then. Just turned fifty, he thought he would go back to his beginnings, to the days when he farmed his father's estate. But this time, everything would be modern and up to date. He would have the first dairy herd on the south coast to be tested for tuberculosis and he would have the biggest tractor. He would farm the place himself with help from relatives. He bought thick corduroys, boots and a cap and set out to be a farmer. Peggy took happy pictures of him digging into the garden with a spade and standing in front of a hay rick that summer of 1920 with his Sussex labourers standing around him. The pictures give an odd

impression of *déjà vu*, as if Paul believed he was still in the fields of
the Ukraine and these sunburned Sussex labourers were really
Ukrainian peasants. The two eldest boys, Nick and Dima,
enrolled as boarders at St Paul's, and Alec, Lionel and George
enrolled as day boys, living with Peggy Meadowcroft during term
time and coming down to Beauchamps in the holidays.

From all corners of Europe, there soon descended on Beau-
champs homeless Russian relatives who had to be taken in; Aunt
Sonia Wassiltchikoff and her husband Boria, who was slowly
dying of tuberculosis contracted in a Bolshevik prison; Uncle
Kolya, the squat red-bearded general in the Preobrajensky
Guards who had left his family behind in the Ukraine; his
son-in-law, the sleek and dapper Colonel Malevsky; and a Judge
Misetsky, whose father had been the family priest in Kislovodsk.
With only two Cordon Bleu lessons behind her Natasha was soon
cooking for twelve Russians at a sitting. When the boys were
home from school, she sent them out to find chestnuts with which
she made *marrons glacés*, bullet-hard concoctions which played
havoc with the judge's false teeth.

For four years, Beauchamps was a crazy Russian circus. Uncle
Kolya was put in charge of the wood lot, and every morning he
would march into the woods, carrying his axe at the slope, military
style, followed by Pug, his faithful Sussex retainer, carrying a
dark blue umbrella. Pug and Kolya spent the whole day in the
woods, laying up fuel for winter and returning at dusk to wash at
the pump. During the boys' holidays from St Paul's, Uncle Kolya
would march them along the country lanes down to Hastings,
singing the Preobrajensky marching song. The boys were with
him once on the sea front at Hastings when the family retriever,
named Jack, relieved himself against a lady seated in a deck chair.
Uncle Kolya knew only two English phrases, and as the lady rose
out of her chair brandishing her umbrella, he tipped his hat,
backed away and used both of them: 'Jack good dog' and 'I love
you.'

Colonel Malevsky was put in charge of a tractor so large for the fields that he could barely turn it at the end of the furrows. Malevsky was enchanted by the tractor but drove it erratically, especially when he had local girls on board. The neighbours got used to pulling a muddy Russian from the ditches, often with a girl underneath.

Judge Misetsky was put in charge of thirty cows. He and the cows did not get on. They would refuse to be milked and he would storm back to the house cursing the English cows for their stubbornness. They would escape and he and Uncle Kolya would have to pursue them through the streets of Battle, once right through the open front door of a sweetshop and out the back.

Every morning, Paul would load the milk cans into the family convertible and make his rounds in the outskirts of Hastings. On school holidays his sons would accompany him, and they were closest then, singing Ukrainian songs as the old automobile rattled down the fragrant English lanes. At every door, Paul would get out, doff his hat and intone in thickly accented English: 'How much milk, madam?'

Every Sunday, they walked to a little church in the wood at the edge of their farm and joined the parishioners in stout Anglican singing.

> In savage lands afar
> Heathen darkness reigneth yet
> Arise O morning star
> Arise and never set.

During term time, the boys learned the English arts of channelling aggression into neatness, politeness and games. Big Dima, gentle, gangling, kindly, made himself into St Paul's boxing champion. Life was harder for his younger brothers, who had to submit to the school regime by day and Peggy's unbending regime by night. Whenever George lost his temper at the boys who jeered at his English and called him – of all things – a 'Bolshie', the masters would take the contending parties down to the school gymnasium and make them settle the matter with boxing gloves. In his misery, George conceived a durable hatred for the English public school, relieved only by a sense of how ridiculous the English could be. There was a master who used to bellow at them, when he caught them sniggering at the back of class. 'The sin of Ham, boy! The sin of Ham!' And what was the sin of Ham? Ham was Noah's son, and he came upon his father sleeping naked in a field, and he laughed. 'And the moral, boy?' the master would bellow. Never laugh at your father's nakedness.

Apart from the holidays at Beauchamps, the boys' other refuge from school and from Peggy was Sunday tea with Uncle Sasha and Aunt Mara Mestchersky in a flat off the Earl's Court Road. Uncle Sasha, Natasha's oldest brother, was a six-foot-six hunchback who went about in a green suit and deerstalker. Aunt Mara was a small onion-shaped woman from the Ukrainian nobility. Sasha and Mara managed to escape in 1920 and came to London, where there was some Mestchersky money, a Mestchersky account at Harrods and a blend of tea in Harrods' food hall called Princess Mestchersky mixture. They had no children and the two of them would pile the Sunday tea table with Russian dishes and watch Natasha's boys, famished from English school food, devour it all. Sasha and Mara lived in a peculiar *ménage à trois* with an old general named Halter, who made a living by forging antique furniture. After tea he would show the boys the little augers he used to make the imitation worm holes. The boys wondered whether there was anything between General Halter and Mara. Much later one of them plucked up the courage to ask and Mara said heavens no, she would die a virgin. She carried her prejudices to the grave, believing, for example, that chimney sweeps were spies for the international Jewish conspiracy.

At half term, George and his brothers would escape from St Paul's and from Peggy and take the train down to the country. Their mother would be at the station to greet them and kiss them and call them by their nicknames and enfold them in their native Russian language. She had learned to sew so that she could replace their buttons and darn their cuffs and she always had a treat for them in the larder. When the oldest ones went to university and came back at the weekends, she had Turkish cigarettes for them and a glass of sherry. Dressed in an old cardigan and a faded striped dress fastened at the neck, Natasha served meal after meal, bringing in the dishes from the kitchen, wandering to and fro, never actually eating, just nibbling on a biscuit or taking a sip of port, listening to her boys chattering and Uncle Kolya and Colonel Malevsky endlessly discussing the disastrous battles of August 1914. Ludendorff's double encirclement of Samsonoff at Tannenberg, the slaughter of the great regiments, still bewitched them and Kolya and Malevsky would refight the battles, with spoons for divisions, knives for batteries, cups for command posts. After the umpteenth refighting of a lost war, Alec, the family tease, asked Kolya what the responsibilities of the Preobrajensky Guards had been.

'To protect the life of the Tsar.'

'Then why didn't you?'

Old Uncle Kolya – I feel for him now – his wife and sons left behind in Bulgaria, reduced to dependence on his brother, once an adjutant general on the Imperial General Staff, now a Sussex woodsman with only Pug for company, gripped the table knife till his knuckles were white and stood up amid a hush and shouted, 'If you were an officer and a gentleman, and not a little schoolboy, I would challenge you to a duel!' Then he was gone, clanking down the passage in his infantryman's boots, slamming the front door, and storming down the gravel path to the woods where he would whittle savagely and brood on the cruelty of children.

That cannot have been the only battle fought at this table between young and old on those school holiday weekends of 1923 and 1924. The first skirmishes in the lifelong disagreement between Nick and his father over the revolution must have occurred here, futile battles about what might have been, with Uncle Boria dying in the upstairs room and Natasha struggling to feed five sons, while the comic-opera troupe of old

Russians whom nobody had the heart to dismiss slowly ate the heart out of the farm.

By then a Miss Isobel Adams Brown had moved in next door. She was a Christian Scientist and a saleswoman for the Spirella Corset Company, and once in her youth she had lived on the Ignatieff estate at Kroupodernitsa as companion to Paul's sister Katia. Hearing the Ignatieffs were in the neighbourhood, she moved in next door and fell in love with Paul. At nights, to escape the menagerie at Beauchamps, Paul would walk up the road to Miss Adams Brown and spend the evening, as he put it, 'doing the accounts'. For company, Natasha turned increasingly to her gynaecologist, a squat little man named Belilovsky who was making a fortune in his London clinic providing heat treatments for Russian émigré women. He would come down by train and listen by the hour as his 'little countess' poured out her troubles: the money just seemed to disappear, the milk round never netted enough, Paul and Miss Adams Brown seemed to spend every night on the accounts, and the boys came home with tearful stories of school and Peggy.

Back at 10A Oxford Road there came a night – some time in 1924 – when Peggy rapped Alec's knuckles with a ruler because he had stumbled over his scales on the piano and he slammed the piano shut and fled the house. He made his way to Belilovsky who went down to Beauchamps to tell Paul that Peggy's regime at 10A Oxford Road must be ended, and that for good measure the little countess was breaking down under the strain of cooking for all the Russians as well.

Peggy had been twenty-one when she appeared at the door of the apartment on Galernaya street in Petersburg in 1911. She gave thirteen years of her life to the family. She found them the ship that took them to safety from Novorossisk and in London she found them a roof over their heads. As the reverent photographs of Count Paul in her photograph album attest, she conceived a hopeless and embittering passion for him which helps to explain the frustration behind her ferocious regime. For his part, Paul always enjoyed the flattery of women's illusions. There was a holiday at Easter in 1922 or 1923 when he took her to the Scilly Isles off Land's End on the Cornish coast with two of the boys, leaving Natasha behind. Paul's seductive and elusive smile beams out at Peggy from the photographs she took of that holiday. She held on to those pictures till the end of her life. Back home in her mother's cramped flat in Putney, locked in the routine of raising boys who were not her own, perhaps missing the ease and contentment of Russia as keenly as the rest of them, still unmarried, still fending off Mr Hough, the ship's officer from the *Huanchaco* who wanted to marry her and who wrote an adulatory article about her bravery in the shipping company magazine, she vented her frustration chiefly on Lionel and George. To this day, the oldest boys speak of her with affection, but that is because they got out early enough. The younger ones still cannot forgive her. They were now removed from 10A Oxford Road and sent to board at St Paul's. They never saw her again.

Back at Beauchamps, Dr Belilovsky's ultimatum to Paul had its effect. The family dispersed. Aunt Sonia took Uncle Boria to Paris. When he died, she established a finishing school for young ladies which she ran until her own death. Uncle Kolya said goodbye to Pug and his woods and went to Bulgaria to find his wife and sons. There he ended his days as a quiet, gloomy librarian in Sofia. Occasionally he would write a mournful letter asking Paul to remember his old brother and enclosing a postcard of him standing beside his grandfather's statue in the public square in Varna. Judge Misetsky left his cows and went back to Poland, taking along an English nurse whom he had met in a Hastings hospital. Colonel Malevsky went to Paris to help in Paul's work with the Russian Red Cross.

Paul himself was absent from Beauchamps more and more. There were not just the evenings with Miss Adams Brown, but now months on end in Paris at the Russian Red Cross. At first he raised money to send medical supplies to the White Russian armies still fighting against the Red armies in Siberia and then, as the civil war ended, for the flood of refugees in the capitals of Europe. For a time, Russian refugees were a popular cause and he had much success with the charitable rich. But then philanthropic attentions began to wander; other causes began to compete, the money began to dry up. He went to see Herbert Hoover, who had been raising money for Soviet famine relief, and the great man told him the plight of the White Russians was 'too stale' for the American public. 'Give me an earthquake or a big flood or some other violent commotion and I would undertake to collect millions in a very short time.' Paul began staying for months at a time in the Hôtel Ramsès in the Square des Batignolles, a dingy square adjacent to a goods yard in northwest Paris. Among the émigré community in Paris he still counted for something. Natasha was left alone at Beauchamps with weekend visits from her boys and Belilovsky.

In the photographs they took of her she is seated on the steps of the old wooden veranda, with her knees up under an old striped frock, always the same one, her hair in an untidy bun, with an aureole of stray grey hairs, her boys around her, laughing soundlessly at a joke or brooding silently in their midst. Increasingly her children protected her as she became more reclusive. When she heard the crunch of a salesman's foot on the gravel or heard Miss Adams Brown or the nosy farming neighbours arriving, she would peek out of the blinds, then steal upstairs to her bedroom and with shooing gestures tell her children to send the intruders away. She bore her hurts in silence: Paul's imperious departures to Paris, his evenings on the accounts with Isobel Adams Brown. When she was fed up with it all, she would lock herself in the bathroom and lie in the bath with a glass of port and mutter to herself.

Paul seemed reconciled to exile, but Natasha continued to ache for the plenty of Russia, for mushrooms in the autumn, for the carpet of wild flowers in the Doughino meadows, for the piles of succulent dill on the market stalls, for the fields of grain. That was what she missed most in the hedged and bordered English countryside, the exuberant, animal plenty of her native land, now in the 1920s starving, verminous, ruined.

Her oldest boys were growing up fast. They towered over her, her five sons, each thin as a rail, each over six feet, loud-voiced, ebullient, melancholy and high-minded like their father. She called them her *durachki* – her little fools. As they became men she teased the seriousness out of them as best she could. She would introduce Nick in company as 'my eldest, in comparison to whom Napoleon was a mere nonentity'. And Vladimir, with his dangling arms, vast drooping face and lopsided grin, she would call 'my little wood violet'. They all had nicknames: Alec was Seyka, Lionel was Lino and George, her youngest, she called Giesenka.

Exile drew her closer to them. In the Caucasus they had seen her transformed into their 'tigress'. Now, greying and in her fifties, she sewed their buttons and kept aside special treats for them when they came home from school, from university, from their first jobs. She cooked and washed for them and became, as she had never been before, the physical heart of their world. And before every journey she would ask them, 'Have you seen to your digestions?'

She and Paul had drummed it into the boys that the past was past and that they must not end up like so many émigrés driving taxis and keeping their bags packed for the return journey to Petersburg. Alec, the family rebel and tease, most like his mother in looks, was the first to leave. In Kislovodsk he had become fascinated with geology and in England completed a degree at the Royal School of Mines. Soon he was off to Sierra Leone to work as an engineer in a gold mine. Nick, the family dreamer and philosopher, wanted to be a writer but his father insisted that he get a degree in something practical, so Nick soldiered his way through a degree in electrical engineering at the University of London. Blanching at the thought of settling in to suburban life, Nick answered an advertisement in a paper offering free passage,

board and lodging to harvesters in Canada, and in 1924 set out
for northern Alberta. Dima soon joined him, lured by Nick's
promise of a job at a lumber camp making railway ties. Nick was a
fantasist and Dima discovered when he arrived that there was no
tie camp and no job. But they stuck it out harvesting and
homesteading in the cold northern plains of Alberta.

Dima came back to England in the autumn of 1927, strong and
sunburned, with stories of riding the boxcars and working in the
endless fields of the prairies which reminded him of the vast
plenty of old Russia. Paul was away all that winter of 1927-28
collecting money for the Red Cross and Dima ran the farm with
Natasha while the younger boys, Lionel and George, completed
their year at St Paul's. By the spring of 1928, Dima was determined to sell the farm. Milk prices were falling and the farm was
too small to be profitable. Some of his former teachers from
agricultural college came up to inspect the place and told him it
was a lovely family home but hopeless as a commercial proposi-
tion. So the twenty-three-year-old Dima ordered the farm to be
sold and wired his father when the deed was done. What is more,
he told his father he was taking his mother and George and
Lionel to Canada. If that was the case, his father replied, then he
would stay on in Paris working for the Red Cross.

To this day, Dima's decision arouses passions. For Dima, the
matter was straightforward: if the farm was losing money, it had
to be sold. For George and Lionel, who could only dimly
remember Russia as a place of terror and deprivation,
Beauchamps was the only home they had ever known. Torn
between a son who was certain the family would go under unless
it made a break for Canada and a husband who was spending
more and more time in the émigré world of Paris, Natasha
decided in favour of her son. George and Lionel watched as the
family wrenched itself apart.

In the early summer of 1928, after the house and farm had
been sold, Dima called in the auctioneers to sell off the contents
of Beauchamps. The valuers came through the house and put

together a catalogue and then a crowd assembled on the lawn and the bidding began. As the hammer rapped down, George and Lionel and Natasha watched their furniture being carted off and the farm animals put into other men's halters and led away. Their own remaining possessions, a tiny heap of clothes and some Russian treasures, were piled once again into Natasha's trousseau trunk and shipped down to Southampton where in September 1928 it was loaded on board the steamship *Montrose*, bound for Montreal. When the ship sailed, George, then fifteen, crawled into bed and held his mother tight to stop her from crying.

They travelled on Nansen passports, issued to stateless refugees. Lionel's and George's were stamped with a Canadian visa admitting them as agricultural labourers. When they landed in Montreal, Dima took George's boater and chucked it into the St Lawrence. 'You won't need that here!' he boomed.

Dima settled them into a cold-water flat in the Victoria Apartments in east-end Montreal. The winter of 1928–29 was a low ebb for Natasha. The money trickled away in that wretched bug-ridden apartment in the icy foreign city, and she was reduced to taking the streetcar down to Bonsecours market to bargain for cheap vegetables to feed her boys. But no matter how little money there was, she sent them to an exclusive private school, Lower Canada College. In order to pay for her sons' education, she gave up spending on herself and began gambling the money from the sale of the farm in penny mining stocks. She entered her sixtieth year, gaunt and bony with deep circles under her eyes, always dressed in the same severe ankle-length black dress fastened at the neck with one of her mother's brooches. Sometime that year Nick came back from Alberta with his fiancée, the daughter of Judge Woods from Edmonton. She remembered meeting Natasha in that dark, narrow apartment in the east end and thinking she was the most mournful and lonesome creature she had ever met in her life.

After a miserable year at school, George set off for the west coast in the spring of 1929 to find a summer job on the railways.

At Grand Central Station in Montreal, Natasha pressed twenty-five dollars into his hand and warned him in her inimitable way that if he got mixed up with 'loose women' his nose would fall off. He was just sixteen and he worked all summer as an axeman on the shores of Kootenay Lake in British Columbia, cutting trees and making stakes for the right-of-way for a railbed linking the Crow's Nest pass with the Kettle Valley Railway line into Vancouver. The railbed skirted the canyon walls of the lake and an axeman had to master his trade one step from a fatal fall. George shed his St Paul's School diction for bunkhouse slang; he picked up an impressive scar on his knee during a duel of axe-throwing with an Irishman and he learned how to fight back when his mates dumped him, bedding and all, into the mountain stream at the back of the camp.

There is a picture in Natasha's album of George on the railbed at the edge of Kootenay Lake that summer of 1929. He has knotted a handkerchief and put it on his head against the heat and he is wearing a work-shirt, jeans and heavy boots. He is arm in arm with two of his workmates and he looks as tough and as happy as they do. They called him the Douk, because the only Russians they had ever met were Doukhobours, members of the reclusive religious sect who had emigrated from Russia and moved into the remote valleys of British Columbia. His boss spent his evenings going through volumes of the *Encyclopedia Britannica*, and one evening came across the article on George's grandfather, Nicholas Ignatieff. When he asked his young axeman whether they were related, George realized he was happier to be thought a decent axeman than to be a count. He came back to Montreal in the autumn, fired up as his brothers had been with the magic of the west and with the feeling that he had proved himself.

Fortunately the stock-market crash of October 1929 saved him from having to return to the pickled gentility of Lower Canada College. Natasha had been trying to stretch their money by buying stocks and when the market collapsed the capital from the sale of Beauchamps was halved. By this time Nick had a job as an electrical engineer with Ontario Hydro and at his instigation the family moved to a rented farmhouse in Thornhill on the northern outskirts of Toronto. The Depression brought the family back together. Dima, who had been homesteading in the Peace River country in northern Alberta, lost his farm to a hailstorm and returned to Toronto to work as a junior instructor in soils chemistry at the University of Toronto. It was his salary that kept the family going in 1930 and 1931.

Then in 1932, Paul arrived from Paris after four years away. The Depression had dried up charitable sources for the Russian Red Cross and so his work had slowed to a trickle. He was now sixty-two and after four years in the little room at the Hôtel Ramsès in the Square des Batignolles it was time to come home. What part he had played in the émigré politics of Paris, that tangled milieu of White plotters and Red *agents provocateurs*, he kept to himself. How Paul explained his absence, how Natasha took him back, neither ever said. They made some sort of peace between themselves and settled into a succession of houses the boys rented for them in Toronto. In the photographs, they always stand a distance apart: he in his rakish fedora, his face a mask of cool charm with the hint of a smile beneath his sweeping moustache; she stooped, squinting, smiling back at the camera, with the choker around her neck and the same spare black dress.

In 1936, Dima found them some land in Upper Melbourne, a small pulp town on the St Francis River in the Eastern Townships south of Montreal, and Paul supervised the building of a little brick two-bedroomed cottage with a screen porch and a high gabled roof to plane away the snow. It stood among the dark pines above the river and they settled in to raise vegetables, to grow a garden and to await the arrival of grandchildren. Natasha continued to play the stock market on the quiet, determined to recoup the losses of 1929. Soon the drawers of her desk were full of prospectuses from companies like White Lake Gold and Porcupine Silver.

George went on a Rhodes Scholarship to Oxford in 1936. His parents did not want him to go, fearing he would be lost to them by settling in England. But his father presented him with General Ignatieff's gold watch and saw him off on the boat. Lionel went to law school at McGill.

In this new country, whose winters recalled their own, whose immensity brought back that lost immensity of their own, Paul and Natasha took out papers of citizenship and were at last able to consign their Nansen passports, emblems of homelessness, to the attic. They were too old by then to shed their accents or to take up new lives but they never tried to clamp their children within an émigré ghetto or to insist on Russian brides. All but one of the sons married outside the Russian circle. When Marjorie Adams, Florence Hargreaves, Helen Fraser and Alison Grant came into the family they stood uncomprehending through their own weddings at the Russian church. One by one the diamond stars on the necklace the Sultan of Turkey had given to the boys' grandmother were taken off and passed along the chain of a now Canadian family. Natasha and Paul bade them all welcome to the family, she with her Garbo voice, he with his courtly attention to the feminine. The Canadian daughters had to get accustomed to Russian directness about all the things which good Canadian Protestants never mentioned in company: digestion, money and grief. These Canadian brides learned how to cook Russian dishes and listened to stories of Kislovodsk and Kroupodernitsa for clues to their husbands' moods – melancholic, hysterical, passionate and withdrawn by turns. All of the sons sought strength and practicality in their wives; they searched for and found in them also their own mother's wry irony.

In September 1939, Nick and Dima enlisted and by 1940 were with the Canadian army in England. Alec was managing explosives factories there, and George was already a junior foreign service officer at Canada House in London. Only Lionel remained behind finishing law school at McGill, living with his parents in the little bungalow in Upper Melbourne, Quebec.

It was some time in the summer of 1940, with her boys overseas and her first grandchildren just arrived, that Natasha began typing out her memoirs in the little wood-panelled bedroom at the back of the bungalow. Paul had written his own memoirs years before in England. He wrote for a public audience; she wrote for her children and grandchildren. My boys, she said, tell me I have a 'special vivid manner of expressing myself. Having no pretensions to authorship, I just do it to please my boys.' She enjoyed herself that summer. Memory, she said, 'quite flew me back to my happy past'.

She used any old scrap of paper she could find – children's exercise books purchased at the Rexall drugstore in town, recipe cards, the back of grocery lists. She typed with two fingers, ignoring punctuation, writing as she spoke, in the English she had learned from governesses at Doughino, the English she knew her grandchildren would grow up speaking as their mother tongue. Back and forth across the years she scavenged, retrieving whatever she could from the darkness. The snow piled high outside in the long winters of the war. She and Paul sat by the fireplace in the sitting room listening to the radio for news of the battles. By 1943, Dima was a chemical warfare officer with the Canadian troops at the battle of Monte Cassino, and Paul and Natasha followed the news of the Italian campaign with painful attention. They listened for all bulletins about Russia, their hearts aching at the names of each town that fell.

I have a picture of them taken by Lionel in the winter of 1944. They are standing outside the cottage in Upper Melbourne, side by side in the snow on a cold winter's afternoon. They are bundled up in long winter coats that seem to pull them down into the earth. Natasha is smiling in that squinting quizzical way of hers. Her grey hair is pulled back in an untidy chignon and her long straight neck is enclosed in a black choker. Her knees are slightly bent and turned inwards, which gives her stance the awkwardness of a shy girl. Paul is standing a fraction apart, elegant as always with an astrakhan perched on his head, a carefully knotted tie and twirled moustaches. The sockets of his eyes are dark and the ridges of his cheekbones are sharp and exposed. He is not smiling. They are both wearing bedroom slippers and they stand on the flagstones, little dry islands in an expanse of white snow. Spring is months off; the darkness will soon close about the house. It is the last picture in the album.

NINE

THE LITTLE FOOLS

Natasha's *durachki*, her little fools, are now old men.

Last summer I went home to Canada to visit them all. Lionel lives in a nursing home north of Toronto. He is in his seventies now and looks like one of the studious saints on an Orthodox icon. I visit him in the Chinese café in a shopping mall many stop lights north of Highway 401, in the featureless sprawl of north Toronto. The café – and the whole mall – are owned by Hong Kong Chinese. Nothing but fields existed here five years ago.

'Hi, Uncle,' the Chinaman says as Lino and I come in. 'This your family from Russia?' 'He's from London,' Lino says slowly. 'You must be happy man, he come see you.' 'I am happy,' Lino says. His legs are bent and he shuffles to a booth and lowers himself down slowly. He wears a pith helmet. He shows me the initials on the hatband and says he checks them to know which way to put it on. He takes the bus to this shopping mall once a month to get his hair cut. 'There is not much to cut,' he says, rubbing his bald head. Afterwards he comes to this café and has tea and almond cookies. It is his major outing.

As a little boy, he grinned madly from the photographs in his father's arms in front of the wicker bathing hut at Misdroy. He is a Mestchersky like his mother but thinner, more finely featured than his brothers. The mad grin of childhood is replaced now by a whisper of a smile. He seems uninterested in the past.

I tell him I've been back to Beauchamps. 'It must be overgrown by now.' He smiles, takes a nibble from the almond cookies. I ask him whether he remembers the view of the sea from his bedroom window. He looks puzzled. 'The sea?'

He says, 'I have something called Parkinson's disease. Do you know about it? It makes my hands shake.' He holds out his spidery hands. His mother's hands. They buzz with a barely perceptible tremor, like current humming through a line. 'I also have had what they call depression. Here,' and he points to a place on the top of his head. 'I received treatments, you know.'

My father had to sign the forms. They put the block between Lionel's teeth; they tied him down, they coursed the current through his limbs. They have stabilized his condition.

'In the hospital I met some exceedingly interesting people, people I would never have met in the world outside. They were depressed too.' This bone-thin traveller, the mildest and gentlest of the brothers, has been in the locked wards. He was the one who paid the price.

'I ask myself many times. What is this depression? I think I know.' He holds his coffee cup between thumb and forefinger and brings it delicately to his lips in a gesture from another time. There is Tina Turner on the radio. He is a long way from Petersburg. He says, 'Depression is not having a purpose in life.'

His brothers say he is the one who was hurt most by exile, by the breaking up of the family in England, by the departure for Canada. He could have stayed in the Russian community in London; he could have continued to be an amateur actor in the dramatic society. Something went wrong. But if his illness is tenacious, so is he. After an early life of false starts – a marriage and a divorce – he got his doctorate and taught Russian literature at Western University in London, Ontario, until his retirement. I tell him I have been reading the Russian poet Anna Akhmatova. He spreads his hands out on the table to watch the tremor. 'In translation. What a pity.'

He looks at me. 'Do you know *The Plain Truth*?' It is an American evangelical magazine. Lino watches evangelical television services from Pasadena, California, every Sunday. My father still takes him to the Orthodox services, but it is the electronic religion of California that has touched him deepest.

'Why were we born?' he asks me. 'Do you know why?'

He should have been a monk: he missed his vocation, he never found a place of retreat. 'We were born of the flesh. We have eaten of the fruit of knowledge. We have been banished from the garden.' Neil Young is on the radio singing, 'I've been searching for a heart of gold.' The Chinese proprietor is tapping his finger on the counter waiting for the fries to fry.

'And why are we here?' Lino asks me. He looks out at a car wheeling around in the parking lot. 'We are here to be sanctified. To be "spiritualized".' He says the word as if he were holding it with tongs. 'To become of the spirit.'

Exile took his purposes away, but now he has found them again. He looks at his watch. It is time to go back to the nursing home for lunch. The nursing home looks like other brown-glass corporate headquarters that squat along the ribbon of highway. In the lobby they are paging someone, and a bell sounds for lunch. Then Lino begins to sing.

> 'In savage lands afar
> Heathen darkness ruleth yet.
> Arise O morning star
> Arise and never set.

'Savage lands *afar*?' he says and looks around the lobby. 'Savage lands *here*!' He lets himself be kissed, shuffles determinedly to the elevator and is gone.

*

Alec and Marjorie Ignatieff's house on Reid Avenue behind the Civic Hospital in Ottawa is a small bungalow ringed by a picket fence on a street of houses much the same as itself. The television is on in the sitting room: Alec sits on the chintz sofa looking at the TV with his good eye. He is terribly thin, grey-faced, his blind eye misted over. Yet for all that he is still the most beautiful of Natasha's children. Eighty years of life have laid the Mestchersky bone structure bare. In the silent and wasted immobility of age, he is still her sailor-suited son. He lets himself be kissed and he says in a whisper, 'I'm going down very fast.' It has been a family joke that he has been going down very fast all his life. Marjorie says of him that he has a richly developed Nunc Dimittis mood. But when I look up, she does not wink as usual.

In a weak voice, he tells me about the Petersburg house, about the warren of corridors which led back to the kitchens and as he does so, he imitates the voices in his memory: '*Grafchiki*' – little count – 'what are you doing in the kitchen? You are gentry, you shouldn't be here!' I see the sweating cook in Fourstatskaya shooing him down the passageway.

When I ask him about Kislovodsk, he tells me about the time he saw a ragged soldier beating a gypsy woman and cursing her over and over: 'You slut, the times of bloody Tsar Nick are over!' He remembers going with his mother to a villagers' hovel outside Kislovodsk in the autumn of 1918 and hearing from inside a parched voice cry, 'Boy, don't come closer. We've got the plague.' It was typhus.

In the fading light of an Ottawa winter afternoon he goes right back to the beginning, to the light of the salon in Kroupodernitsa. It is 1910. He has been reprimanded by Aunt Mika because he has mispronounced something. What is it? He searches, bends his head. Aunt Mika was giving him his Bible lesson, getting him to repeat the words of the Gospel when Christ appears before Pilate. Alec was four: he kept pronouncing Pontius like *ponchiki*, the word for brioche. Then he was turned by his shoulders and placed in the corner. His clear eye stares out across time: 'I watch through the window as the light fades to the left. A darkening sky.' His words come out blurred, like a page of writing left out in the rain. Then there is silence, filled by the television news at six o'clock and the clicking of teacups. His memory reminds me of a film of an undersea wreck: here and there, amid the silt and gloom, there is a broken bottle, a shard, a doubloon.

He was the rebel son. 'She wasn't kissable,' he says of Natasha.

[169]

'Sometimes she would kiss us on the forehead. She would sit Lionel and George on her knees. I'm damn sure I was never on her knees.' He was the one who got out of 10A Oxford Road first, the one who slammed down his fists on the piano and refused to play another of Peggy Meadowcroft's infernal exercises. He went to the Royal School of Mines, to tin mines in Cornwall, gold mines in Sierra Leone. The mines were right for him: the solitary one of the family, down in the earth, bent double in those dark shafts. After the war he came to Canada and ran the Department of Mines in the Ministry of Energy.

Alec is silent so his wife says, 'He was always the odd one out in the family.' 'Why are you marrying this bad character?' were Paul's first words to Marjorie when Alec presented his bride to his father. 'He was too hard on his sons,' she says with a look of pain in her face. Alec laughs, a dry harsh laugh. Silence. I get up to go. With great effort he levers himself up. He used to be several inches taller, a thin giant at six foot four. Now I am taller than he is. I kiss him on his forehead.

In the driveway, Marjorie squeezes my hand and says, 'You came too late.'

*

I have a picture of Nick – the oldest brother – on horseback somewhere out west in the 1930s, tall and easy in the saddle, elegant in jodhpurs and a suede jacket, the sun lighting the high forehead, the deep eyes in shadow and an expression of irritation on his face as if he resents the camera's intrusion. He wanted to be a writer, but he made himself an electrical engineer to please his father. When he lost his job in the Depression, it came as a great release. He set off with a backpack through the bush country of northern Ontario, through little mining towns like Timmins and Cochrane, then across the prairies on the freights with the men who rode the rails in search of work. He wrote articles urging the opening up of the north for immigrant settlers, he wrote about the hobos he met on the rails and he thought of those months on the road as the happiest of his life. He slept under the stars by the northern lakes, in freight cars, on the front sofas of missionaries who combed the freight yards trying to convert the waifs and strays. He lived on a diet of raisins and bread, fruit and coffee. Tall, sunburned, athletic, slightly balding, with a natural authority that made him seem older than his years, he had a knack for making influential friends, for ending up in first class. His brothers in Toronto laughed when they got a telegram from their hobo brother telling them to put his dinner jacket on the first train north to Cochrane. He had met the president of the railroad at one of those northern sidings and the president had invited him to travel in his private car. All the way round Lake Superior, the big man smoked his cigars and listened while the young Russian poured out his schemes to open up the north to immigrant settlers. Nick was a man of schemes and dreams and speeches and projects and he always acted as if he was playing on a larger stage than the one he was actually on.

All of his life was a long reckoning with the Soviet experiment and with the failure of the beliefs and hopes his father had lived by. In 1936 he wrote an article for *Saturday Night* magazine in Toronto in praise of Stalin's new Soviet constitution. He tried to defend terror, forced collectivization and the purges as the birth agony of a new society. In the coming war with Hitler, he said, Russia would be our ally again. It was always Russia he saw, eternal and unchanged beneath the carapace of the Soviet regime. His father thought him sentimental and naive and wrote a reply to the article saying so.

'"Land to the peasants! Peace! Soldiers back to our homes!" Where are those promises now?' Paul wanted to know. 'The land belongs to the state; the collective farms are run by outsiders belonging to the new bureaucracy; the peasant is enslaved more than ever; while more soldiers are under colours now than ever before and the entire nation is militarized.' Paul signed his reply, which *Saturday Night* published, 'Your loving father and friend'.

Nick replied, 'There is nothing more futile than to belong to a class which learns nothing and forgets nothing.' And signed his reply, 'Your otherwise respectful son Nicholas'.

When World War II came Nick served in the Russian section of British intelligence in London. Once he was sent to Buckingham Palace to brief the King, George VI, on the new Soviet ally. As the war progressed he became ever more disillusioned with the way the Allied intelligence community came to withhold military information from the Soviets, and he argued fiercely with his brother George over the need to trust and assist their Russian brothers-in-arms. George was always more circumspect than his brother about the Soviets.

After the war, Nick returned to a wife he hardly knew and a son he had never seen. A solitary moody man, hard to live with, hard to forget, he became warden of Hart House at the University of Toronto, helping ex-soldiers like himself to return to the university, lecturing and writing all the while on Soviet affairs, fighting as best he could the McCarthyite tide of anti-Soviet hysteria. In March 1952 he was lecturing the Defense Staff College in Kingston on Soviet strategic intentions, insisting – in the wake of the news that the Soviets had the H-bomb – that a nation bled white by war had no interest in military aggression against the West. Again and again, he came back to the theme of the essential continuity between the autocracy of old and new Russia; the anti-Western Slavophilism of his grandfather, he said, was echoed in the Communist ideology of capitalist encirclement. He was already at work on a book to be called *The Eternal Crisis – Russia and the West*.

On 27 March 1952, he gave his annual speech to the students in the Great Hall of Hart House. By then, Russia past and present suffused his thoughts. He began his speech by recalling an autumn afternoon in 1918 when he had sat on a hillside in the Caucasus and had watched the Red and White armies in the valley below killing each other for possession of Kislovodsk:

I was then fourteen . . . I remember thinking acutely for the first time: what pitiful fools these grown men are to do this to each other on a day like this in a place like this. What blasphemy. All through those months and years of stress, excitement, misery, I was disturbed and refused to accept the authority of the explanations handed down to me by my elders and betters . . . When my father and all our friends and relations said that Communism could only be fought by force and even to hang Communists was a service to society, I could not see the point and was haunted by the spectacle of a young mother who happened to be an active Communist and wife of one of their captured leaders, hanging for three days from a gibbet erected on a hill in the middle of the town.

I often wonder why this memory of the gibbet on the hill came back to him that night, why it seemed to fuel his sense of suffocation at the McCarthyism around him, the parochialism of student politics, the numbing geniality of Toronto life. Next afternoon, he was changing a tyre in the parking lot at the base of Hart House tower. He had a heart attack and died instantly. He was forty-eight, an elusive romantic haunted by a country he never lived to see again.

*

From a phone booth in the echoing concourse of Montreal's Grand Central Station, I call Dima and tell him my train will be arriving at Richmond in an hour and a half.

'All present and correct to meet you, boy!' His voice booms: I hold the receiver away from my ear. The other brothers call him the Prefect.

The train journey from Montreal to Richmond winds south-west across the St Lawrence River through small brick sunlit towns called St Hyacinthe and Acton Vale, where now, on an August afternoon, men start sharing out the beer and lighting the

[173]

barbecue and kids in Expo sweatshirts play scratch games on the lawns among the sprinklers. These towns are more French than they were in Natasha's time: all the signs which used to say Hardware now say Dépanneur, and the train man calls the names of the stops in French. In the car, the families down for a day's shopping in Montreal are munching potato chips and some of the children are asleep on their parents' laps. The fathers work in the Bombardier skidoo factory, in the asbestos mines at Thetford and on the dairy farms that dot the soft rolling countryside. The corn is ripening, the cows are wending their way to the barns.

When I smell the sulphur from the Windsor Mills pulp plant and catch my first glimpse of the St Francis River and the railway bridge I know we are nearly there. Dima brought Paul and Natasha here in 1936 to a little brick bungalow they built on the shores of the St Francis on land sold to them for a dollar by F. M. Robinson, the farmer for whom Dima had worked when he first came to Canada.

From the window of the train I see Dima striding up the platform searching the windows for my face and tapping the train windows with his stick. His hair is like steel wool and it rises straight up on the crest of his head; he is crooked like a great tree and he is wearing an extraordinary pair of bright green corduroy shorts. He is eighty-two years old. I tap on the window and he does a welcoming dumb-show, waving his stick and blowing me a kiss. When I step down on the platform he kisses me on the lips and bellows, 'Say, it is good to see you, boy!'

They all know him here, the taxi drivers waiting for their old ladies back from a day's shopping, the retired schoolteacher waiting for his wife, the stationmaster with the packet of express mail for Sherbrooke down the line. He is a kind of local seigneur, living in the big house on the edge of town, taking the annual salute at the Canadian Legion parade on Remembrance Day. He waves his stick at them all and directs Florence to drive us home.

Florence wears her glasses on a chain and drives hunched forward grasping the wheel tightly and squinting at the road. She keeps him going, keeps his voice down to bearable levels, teases him off his certainties and reminds him that he's told the same story before.

The car pulls off the highway up the curving driveway to Beechmore, a three-storey, steeply-gabled Victorian house with high ceilings and numberless rooms, a big kitchen where the wood stove burns all day and night and deep-carpeted rooms where the clocks tick on white marble mantelpieces. The house was built in the 1860s: there is a mezzotint of Sir Wilfred Laurier in the hall and the furniture was made for the house out of Quebec maple 100 years ago. It is a house of the same size and vintage as 'Beechums'. The bungalow where Paul and Natasha used to live was directly across the river: it has long since been sold. Beechmore is now the family's gathering place.

After downing his vodka and hot water and making himself comfortable in the huge armchair which has been built up to accommodate his gigantic size, Dima takes the notebook from my hand and draws the floor plan of the house at Kroupodernitsa, every room, every corridor, marking with an X the hole in the dining room wainscot where Alec and he would hide the Jerusalem artichokes they hated but their grandmother commanded them to eat. Dima's return to this house he has not seen since Easter 1915 is effortless. He remembers everything as if it were yesterday: Mitro the coachman and the morning rides with his grandmother through the lanes of the estate; the servant girls carrying the steaming cauldrons of jam to cool on the veranda steps; the way his grandmother used to crack walnuts between her teeth and hand her grandchildren the pieces. To Dima it seems the most natural thing in the world that through the transmission of his memory to me, I am joined in time with a woman who dined with Disraeli, wearing the Sultan's stars.

I ask him why he never went back to Petersburg. He will not have anything to do with Bolsheviks. 'The bastards,' he says with relish. He has kept faith with his mother's convictions.

In the dining room, Florence serves us dinner from heavy

silver dishes and she laughs when she recalls how Paul and Natasha would drive in together from Upper Melbourne to Richmond to do the shopping in the Buick they called Sweet Mary. Natasha would sit upright in the middle of the back seat in her hat and gloves and choker, and Paul would drive very slowly, tipping his fedora and bowing his head ever so slightly at the old ladies he passed in the street: '*Bonjour Madame*,' he would say out of the window.

Natasha used to bargain with the butcher in Richmond, the mild-mannered Mr Duluth. 'Robber! *Cochon!* That's too much! I won't pay that!' None of his customers had ever tried to bargain with Mr Duluth before and he rather liked it. In some region of her mind, she was still at the Ohotniki Riad in the old Arbat in Moscow. He got to like the game, and once when Florence came in with Paul and paid his price without complaining, the butcher looked startled, then winked at Paul and said, 'The young one's not like the old one, is she?'

Natasha loved to rummage in the Rexall drugstore, particularly in the one-cent sale tubs, and she stocked up on soap, toilet paper and laxatives as if preparing for a siege. There was never enough money: something from Dima and Florence every month, an old American insurance policy that had matured, and a tiny bit extra which she used to put on the mining stocks. Her boys teased her about her stock market gambling, but she took it very seriously and managed to recoup every cent lost in the crash of 1929.

She was famous for her conversations on the party line with the few local friends she made: Mrs Moray, the Swiss doctor's wife, or Mrs Trigg, the bank manager's wife. Whenever her neighbours on the party line heard the tell-tale click that announced she had come on the line, they would pick up their receivers and hear her say her cleaning lady was 'fat as five cows', or hear her call herself 'the old crow'.

I want to know whether my grandparents were happy in Canada. Florence says, 'He was happy, I think.' Paul worked the garden every day of spring and summer, growing kohlrabi and beetroot, digging the earth with a pitchfork, in rubber boots and an old cardigan, an old Russian gentleman with a distinguished moustache and a battered fedora for garden use. In the winters, he sat with Mr Trigg, the retired bank manager, and worked on a translation of those even, sifted memoirs he had written sometime in the 1920s.

And Natasha? Florence knows what it is like here in the winter when the snow reaches the windowsill and every book has been read twice and for conversation you have to rely on Dima and your tender-hearted but slow-witted housekeeper. 'You're fighting negative thoughts all the time. I mean, why not just give up?'

Then Dima says, 'Just before I went overseas in 1940, I came back for the weekend to say goodbye and my mother took me aside and said, "We must get out of here."' The winters were too hard and lonely: she was perishing for lack of stimulation. All her sons were far away and she wanted to go out to Vancouver, where the weather was better and where she could be near Lionel, who was teaching school. Dima was furious. 'I had brought them here, helped them to build the house. I refused, I told her they must stay there.' He wants to explain, then he is silent for a time. 'You see, that was the last time I ever saw her.'

They say good night and leave me rummaging among the family papers stored upstairs in the bare rooms under the eaves. It is all a jumble, too confused for any sorting: Natasha's and Paul's Nansen passports with terrible strained photographs of both of them; Paul's bills from the hotel in the Square des Batignolles; correspondence in Russian from the Azov bank relating to his vanished industrial estates; even the catalogue for the sale of the house contents at Beauchamps, with a price in some auctioneer's neat and pitiless hand beside every item. Sitting there at the top of a sleeping house, my hands black with dust from the documents, I wonder what possesses me to rummage through these traces of their mortality, why I must cover my hands with dust from the tomb of their dispossession.

When I come down to breakfast the next morning, Aunt Florence is in the kitchen making toast. She is talking about the times she used to visit Paul and Natasha during the war. 'It was never Stalin or Hitler. Oh no. She always referred to them as Beast Stalin and Mad Dog Hitler. She would come down to breakfast and you would ask her what was on the news and she would say briskly, "They've shot down 189 of those beastly planes of Mad Dog Hitler, thank God."'

All through the war, Paul and Natasha felt a painful closeness to the course of the battle in the Soviet Union. A nephew, Nicholas Mestchersky, was one of those members of the White émigré community in Paris who believed after the fall of France that their best hope of a return to power in Russia lay in joining the German army and fighting on the Eastern Front. He died in the snow on the edges of Leningrad, wearing a German lieutenant's uniform. Paul's cousin Alexis Ignatieff had returned from Paris to Moscow and was lecturing at the Soviet army staff college and advising the military tailors who were reintroducing the epaulettes and shoulder flashes worn by the old Tsarist regiments into the Soviet army. In his apartment in Moscow his batman would answer the phone: 'General Count Citizen Ignatieff at your service!' The family renegade, he had tired of the hatred of the émigré community for having backed Lenin in 1917 and sometime in the 1930s he returned to Stalin's Russia. The Kremlin made him a general and used him to bring back spit and polish and old-style drill. They even let him write his memoirs: *Fifty Years in the Service*. In the book, he dealt ironically with his poor cousin Paul, once a minister, once a millionaire, now 'eking out his old age in poverty, supporting himself by the produce of his garden which he actually works himself, in far-off Canada'.

As Germans and Russians slaughtered each other at the gates of Kiev, Paul must have thought constantly about his sister Mika, last heard from in the summer of 1918 alone in the path of the German army, and now again – in her sixties if she was still alive – in the path of an invading army. Then against all odds, in the middle of the war, they received a picture of her, out in the snow carrying a load of wood with a peasant woman beside her: Mika has turned and is smiling at the camera. How Paul must have stared at the picture of his sister, lost behind the veil of war, her hair grey now like his, her skin worn like his, flesh of his flesh irremediably out of reach, yet transmitting like a distant star the message she knew would mean most to him and which she scribbled in pencil on the back of the postcard: 'They have not forgotten the village choirmaster.'

There were grandchildren by then – Paul and Mika – brought down to visit by their mother Florence. Their grandfather towed them in sleighs and their grandmother made them Russian yoghurt sugared with maple syrup, and at night when they cried out in their sleep their grandfather would come to them and they would hear him say: 'Is this a little bird I hear?' in his thick old Russian voice.

After breakfast, Dima leads the way up the stairs into the attic over the garage. The floorboards and the walls are made from massive rough-hewn planks – the unconsidered forest magnificence that grew on this site a century ago. We pick our way past boxes of children's clothes, old suitcases, toolboxes and saw-horses, spare lumber. At the end of the attic, lit by the cobwebbed light of the dormer window, stands a battered canvas trunk the shape of a loaf of Hovis bread, bound with leather straps. Her initials: NM for Natasha Mestchersky, the childhood self, then NI, the adult self, are visible on the top and when I shoo away the dust, all the stopping places of exile show up on baggage markings: a Canadian Pacific sticker for the 'ss *Montrose*: Countess Natasha Ignatieff, Montreal, Not Wanted on the Voyage'; then in pencil on a sticker, '10A Oxford Road, Putney'; then in faint but legible blue chalk – like words seen in a dream – 'Kislovodsk via Mineralni Vodi'. We open up the top: the lining is white linen stretched on cane and on the inside lid there is the maker's stamp, E. Deraisme, 729 rue St Honoré, Paris, 1902. It is quite empty.

It is as if I have followed a river course along an arduous climb and found at last the bubbling cleft from which the water springs. This is the source of all we became in Canada: everything from that other life which has haunted me since childhood was in this trunk, the icons, the embossed volumes of Karamzin's history, the square silver basin and the ewer in which my great-grandmother used to wash her hands every morning at Dough-ino; the photograph albums, the Sultan's stars. All of this has flowed from the trunk down the branching capillaries of a family that now stretches out from here to Australia, to England, to New Mexico and that still has branches, unknown, on Russian soil. Dima remembers the trunk going on board *La Flandre* in Constantinople harbour in June 1919, how the Turkish stevedore's legs trembled, how he sweated as he wobbled up the gangplank – all the weight of that past teetering on the brink of its passage to the present. But it made it: all the voyages of eighty years now make a circle back to me: Nice to Kroupodernitsa, to Petersburg, to Kislovodsk, to Novorossisk, to Constantinople, to London, to Montreal, to the lumber room of an attic in Richmond, Quebec.

Dima and I set off after lunch up the hill to the cemetery. In the fields the light skims over the top of the waving grain; on the rutted path he reaches over for a stalk of barley, takes the head and works the kernels loose with his fingernails. He was a soils chemist by training, a scientific farmer as his father had been. For thirty years Dima was a soils expert with the Food and Agricultural Organization, trying to improve the yields of rice paddies and peasant plots throughout Asia and Africa, issuing voluble instructions about nitrogens and phosphates and the dangers of night soil in the food chain, leading singsongs of 'Alouette' at all the parties, *Oncle Merde* to his French colleagues.

'Would you rather have been a farmer?' I ask as he studies the barley. He shakes his head. 'You have to be a mechanic, and you have to manage cheap labour. I would have been happy a hundred years ago.' I laugh: 'With the serfs.'

He points his finger at me, and his eyebrows arch: 'They weren't slaves, boy.'

'Just people you could count on.'

'Exactly.'

He resumes walking: his vigorous, bent gait, the huge feet and hands and the tapping stick rolling forward. 'None of this damn modern stuff.'

'Equality, you mean.'

'That's it, none of this damn equality.'

He walks on in front of me, shouting over his shoulder as he goes, 'I always knew I was a count. I always knew I had to take charge.' He always took charge, this old man who conserves intact the open cheerfulness of a twelve-year-old boy.

St Andrew's Presbyterian cemetery stands on a sloping hill high above the St Francis River. Dima is on the cemetery committee and he checks that they keep the grass trim and the cypresses against the skyline shaped and fertilized. A highway has been built to within 100 yards of the back fence and the occasional whine of a passing car makes him fret. For me it seems quiet and unchanged. All my memories flow together into one impression of the light upon the solid Presbyterian names cut into the marble, the cypresses at the top of the walk, the warm breeze off the fields and the glint of the river's course below.

Theirs are the only Russian names in the cemetery: 'In loving memory, Count Paul Ignatieff, 1870–1945; Countess Natasha Ignatieff, 1877–1944.' They share the same stone, the same earth. There is a large plot of grass around them. Dima spreads his hands out and indicates where our plots are: there is room for everyone, even for me. And then for an instant he seems old and frail. He makes the sign of the cross, and he says, 'And this, my dear boy, is where I join them.'

*

In August 1944, my father came back from London. He had been away nine years. He had left for England in 1936 to study at Oxford as a Rhodes Scholar. He had been to Bulgaria to research a thesis about his grandfather and Tsarist policy in the Balkans; he filled folders with research notes; he saw his grandfather's statue in Varna's main square and spent long hours with his Uncle Kolya, finishing his days as a librarian in Sofia. He had been to Nuremberg, Munich and Vienna in the summer of 1938 and had seen fascism first hand. In 1940 and 1941 he fire-watched on the roof of Canada House in Trafalgar Square and organized the evacuation of London children on the transport ships. He had been to the hospitals in 1942 to visit the Canadian soldiers back from the massacre at Dieppe. He had met and fallen in love with my mother. He was a boy when he left for England; in 1944 he returned to his parents a man.

When he arrived in Montreal, his father said he should come down to see them in Upper Melbourne as quickly as he could. The old man's voice sounded rattled. When George came into Natasha's bedroom, the cedar-panelled refuge looking out over the row of pines and the bright August fields, she said immediately in her deep voice, 'Here I am in my bed dying.'

Nick's wife Helen was with him and they sat Natasha up in bed and bathed her. The bones on her chest stood out unbearably, and there were deep cavities under her cheekbones. She was light as a child to lift, bright-eyed, feverish. In all those years of feeding others, she never seemed to feed herself. She would wander in and out of the kitchen, serving her men, nibbling on a biscuit or a prune, sipping from a glass of port, never joining in the eating. She was afraid of dying of cancer like her mother, and she believed cancer arrived in what she ate. So she ate as little as she could and now she was dying among other things of malnutrition, dying of her fear of cancer.

George sat up all night with her. Poised there, at the lip of unconsciousness, holding his hand, with the comical, heart-aching directness that was always hers, she told him the most intimate secrets of her marriage: It was not his fault. I could not make him happy. Never blame your father. The blame is mine.

Mamenka, mamenka.

She confessed a sinful wish to die, to die before her husband. Her wish was granted.

They buried her in the cemetery on the hill overlooking the river on a bright August afternoon. Dima and Nick were still away at the war and Lino was in British Columbia, but George and Helen and Florence were there with all the people in Richmond and Upper Melbourne who had come to know them. Even Mr Duluth, her butcher, came and stood on the other side of the cemetery gate with his hat in his hands.

When Paul was left alone, his daughter-in-law Helen went to live with him in the cottage through the autumn and winter of 1944–45. She called him Jedda. He called Helen his black beauty and there can be little doubt he bloomed in the presence of his tall dark-haired daughter-in-law, who skied into town when the cottage was snowbound and who shared with him the bright cheerfulness of her baby son, Nicholas. Once Paul told her about the time he went with his father to the Cossack villages in the Caucasus mountains to buy wild horses from the tribesmen. But that was all, just that story. He was not one to reminisce. In the spring he put on his old fedora and his cardigan and planted out his kohlrabi. He kept Natasha's garden weeded and her phlox and delphinium came up in abundance in August.

The night before the war with Japan ended in August 1945, my father was sitting with his father listening to the radio. The bombs on Hiroshima and Nagasaki had been dropped. A man born in the Russian ambassador's house above the Bosphorus in 1870, a man who had been treated by Charcot and had served the last Tsar of all the Russias, had arrived in the estuary of the new age. My father looked out the window at the darkening light among the pines and heard his father say that the Japanese would never surrender unless guarantees were given about retaining the Emperor. It was with remarks such as these that they were closest, son and father, never talking about each other, but always about the news. My father turned to say that he thought he was right. His father's breathing had ceased.

*

Paul and Natasha died two years before I was born.

Someone once said devotion to the past is one of the disastrous forms of unrequited love. Like all loves mine feeds and grows on impossibilities. When I look at their final photographs in the family album, standing in front of the bungalow on a snowy afternoon, I want to be there to walk with them up the path to the house, to help them out of their coats, to make them a cup of tea and sit with them by the fire. I want to hear them speak, I want to feel the warmth of their hands.

Any love has its ambivalences, its feelings of suffocation. When I was younger, I wanted to be free of the unending stare of their portraits. But I also wanted them to mark out the path ahead, to help me make my choices, to guide me on the road. Now I have children and a family of my own and I have learned that you can inherit loyalties, indignation, a temperament, the line of your cheekbones, but you cannot inherit your self. You make your self with your own hands, here and now, alone or with others. There is no deliverance, no imperative in the blood. You cannot inherit your purposes. I know what I cannot have from Paul and Natasha and so we are reconciled.

I do not believe in roots. When Natasha was a little girl she believed she was a green shoot on a great tree descending into the dark earth. But I am the grandchild of her uprooting, the descendant of her dispossession. I am an expatriate Canadian writer who married an Englishwoman and makes his home overlooking some plane trees in a park in north London. That is my story and I make it up as I go along. Too much time and chance stand between their story and mine for me to believe that I am rooted in the Russian past. Nor do I wish to be. I want to be able to uproot myself when I get stuck, to start all over again when it seems that I must. I want to live on my wits rather than on my past. I live ironically, suspicious of what counts as self-knowledge, wary of any belonging I have not chosen.

I have not been on a voyage of self-discovery: I have just been keeping a promise to two people I never knew. These strangers are dear to me not because their lives contain the secret of my own, but because they saved their memory for my sake. They beamed out a signal to a generation they would never live to see. They kept faith with me and that is why I must keep faith with them and with those who are coming after me. There is no way of knowing what my children will make of ancestors from the age of dusty roads and long afternoons on the shaded veranda deep in the Russian countryside. But I want to leave the road marked and lighted, so that they can travel into the darkness ahead, as I do, sure of the road behind.

AFTERWORD

━━━

The paved road had given out many miles back and the Moskvitch sedan was now picking its way among the ruts and up-ended cobbles of a farm road in the dark. It was a clear cold night in October and we were in south-central Ukraine, but only the driver, who said nothing, seemed to have any idea where we were. For an hour, the road had been winding through featureless fields bereft of hedges or trees. On the outskirts of an industrial town called Pogribisce, we had passed a factory, working at night, sending up plumes of steam into the air. I had fallen asleep and had just woken again as the car pitched down a steep hill and bumped over some railway tracks, gleaming in the dark between a pair of low white-washed barns. The Moscow-Odessa line, the driver said. After crossing the railway tracks, the farm road led down between steeply sloping stony fields towards a clump of trees. The car's headlights sprayed beams down into the valley below and picked up a silvered dome amidst the trees. At the bottom of the hill, the road petered out into a cleared space in front of a churchyard gate. We stopped and Lena, my translator, and I got out. The driver lit a cigarette and waited. Not a dog's bark. Just the deep silence of the countryside at night and the stars through the trees above my head. I knew where I was.

My father and I had talked about coming here together. In the summer of 1983, we had arrived in Kiev and he had mentioned the village's name to the tour guide and asked how far it was. It was far, we were told, and roads were bumpy and you couldn't make it back to Kiev by nightfall and there was nowhere to stay when you got there. As far as my father was concerned, that was that. The place didn't mean anything much to him – he had never actually been there, only his brothers had – and I didn't press the point, though I knew he was being disingenuous. By the time we reached Kiev, we had already been to Petersburg and he was tired. He had only been six years old when he left Russia: it was all behind the veil. There was almost nothing for him to hold on to. The effort to remember anything at all had left him feeling exhausted and somehow bereft. On the day we had left Petersburg, he sat by the train window with my mother. Later she told me that he looked out at the city of his birth sliding by, then blurring, then disappearing and he suddenly began to cry.

In August 1989, six years after the trip to Petersburg, he went back to Richmond, Quebec, to visit his brother Dima and his wife, Florence. These visits had their rituals: every time he went, he drove past the pine-shadowed bungalow where his mother and father had lived the last years of their lives; he drove up to the cemetery on the ridge and stood there, just by the low iron gate and looked at his parents' graves; he spent a few days reminiscing with Dima and Florence, sitting together on lawn chairs in front of the big Victorian house called Beechmore. My brother was there and he says my father was in good spirits. One day, the town doctor stopped by to pay Dima a call, and while he was there, my father asked the doctor to listen to his heart. He said he'd felt short of breath carrying in the groceries that morning. Doctor Cormier put his stethoscope to my father's heart and went to the phone and dialled a number. An ambulance came and took him to the Sherbrooke General Hospital, and my father died there – alone, in an intensive care unit – of a multiple heart attack in the early hours of 10 August 1989. He died in the same hospital as his mother, and my brother and

I buried him next to his parents on the ridge overlooking the St Francis River.

Now, four years later, I was standing in the dark by the churchyard in the middle of the Ukraine, and it seemed that I was resuming the journey my father and I had started, but never completed.

Even in the dark, I had an intense sense of knowing where I was. The Russian Album had guided me home. It was as if the photographs had lodged their faint and fading outlines in my mind as a memory of my own. I was certain, for example, that the barns on either side of the railroad tracks had been built by my great-grandfather. There would have been a small station at the top of the road, where the Moscow-Odessa express would stop, and my great-grandfather's newspapers and mail would have been handed to the station porter, who in turn would have handed them to my grandfather, then in his teens, who would have tossed them onto the seat beside him and driven back, in the two-wheeler, down the very hill I had just travelled to deliver them to his father, taking his morning's tea on the veranda of the great house. Now I stood by the green gates of the village church he had built in the 1880s, a small-scale brick imitation of Santa Sophia in Sofia, its brick outlines and lead domes just visible behind a line of pine trees ringing the graveyard.

Opposite the church, behind some ragged picket fences, were three small brick cottages, with lights on through curtained windows, but we stood there in the dark, by the churchyard, not knowing which one to approach. Then a flatbed truck clattered down the hill and drew up and stopped, spilling saucers of light on the trees and the graves in the churchyard. The driver looked the three of us over, me, my translator, Lena, and my driver, and told us to jump in. We clambered up into his cab and he drove us slowly through the narrow, unpaved track that meandered through the village, the sides of the truck brushing heavily against the vegetation which hung over the low wooden fences on either side. He stopped in front of a blue and white brick house, almost covered with vines, and banged on the door. After many minutes, a burly priest with a full grey beard unbolted the door and stood under the single bulb at his doorway, irritably wiping crumbs from his cassock. What did we want? Lena kissed his hand and explained. The priest looked surprised, then suspicious: one of the family? In the middle of the night? Lena said, indeed it was. He stood there, not quite knowing what to do with us, until his wife, in kerchief, carpet slippers and a coat thrown over her house dress led us back down the path through the village to a cottage, where, she said, we would sleep. She led us in, lit candles, pointed Lena in one room, me and the driver in the other room, plumping pillows, dragging furniture about, blowing on the coal fire, until the Dutch oven heated up and began to take the chill from the room. She lit the lamps in front of the icons in the corner, as well as the coal lamps on the tables, and bustled about in the kitchen, while we sat and felt the warmth rising in the room. Tea and a soup tureen full of potatoes, jars of pickled tomatoes, onions and cucumbers, several bottles of vodka and some cognac appeared on the red-and-white-checked oil skin table-cloth. She laughed and chuckled and showed her bright-silver false teeth and acted as if she had been waiting for us to show up one day.

When her husband appeared, he had combed his hair, brushed away the crumbs and was wearing his silver cross over his cassock. He blessed the feast now assembled on the trestle table and his wife joined in, crossing herself, bowing and warbling the responses in an old lady's quaver. We bowed too and sat down at the table. You must eat, you must eat, she kept saying, stabbing the gherkins in the jar with a fork and shaking them onto our plates. Her husband, with his silver cross now around his neck, was circumspect, watching me closely through small eyes, moving his fingers around his lips beneath his beard. Was this really the Count's grandson?

I explained, through Lena, that my father had been a believer all his life, and an elder of his church. They were reassured by the thought that there were islands of faith in Manning Avenue, Toronto and other unimaginable places. They were too polite to ask about my own beliefs, but it seemed clear to them – from the fact that I had no Russian, that I didn't cross myself properly at grace, merely bowed my head – that in the spiritual department I was something of a disappointment. And this was not the place to rehearse the evident contradiction between having sought out this village while, at the same time, keeping a psychological distance from Russian traditions. Now that I had found the village at last, I felt a comical desire to lie: to drink more vodka than I ordinarily like, to tell Russian stories (with Lena's help, of course), to cross myself with ostentatious correctness and in every respect conceal the fact that I was not really very Russian at all. In planning this sentimental journey, I had prepared myself to be disappointed; what I had not prepared myself for was the possibility that *they* might be disappointed in me. The priest's wife looked at me commiseratingly. So why hadn't I learned Russian? Because, I said, my father married a Canadian woman. But it's the language of your father, the priest said. Which was exactly why I never learned it. But how could I tell him that?

Fortunately there was Lena. They couldn't make out what she was to me exactly, but her Russian was expressive and faultless and she obviously had a warm heart and was respectful too, and they began to unwind in our company. Vodka was poured into tumblers from a large fruit jar in which were floating several green peppers and a gherkin or two. While his wife kept piling the potatoes and sausage on our plates, and joining in with asides, commentary and corrections, Father Sergei told his story. When they arrived to take over the parish, in the early years after Stalin's death, the church was boarded up and the machine shop for the collective farm stood in the churchyard. 'There was a butcher shop in the crypt,' his wife added, 'can you imagine?' They pulled the boards off the windows and swept out the cobwebs, dust and animal droppings on the mosaic floor and re-lit the candles and began holding services, and the old widows began coming again and brought their daughters and their sons. And soon there were baptisms, as well as burials, and a choir to sing in the loft. The priest and his wife had sons, and the boys joined the choir and then left for the seminary to train for the priesthood. But it had never been easy. The priest had been arrested more than once, but he didn't want to talk about it. 'We are still here,' he said phlegmatically, chewing on a piece of black bread, looking down at the table. 'We have kept your graves,' she said and smiled, her silver false teeth flashing, while her husband looked sharply at me, wondering, it seemed to me, why I was worthy of such unrewarded devotion.

To release myself from his stare, I asked him – through Lena – how things had fared for them and for the church since the Ukrainians had declared independence in 1991. They both exchanged a worried glance. It was like this, the priest said. A new Ukrainian Church, with support from the state, was demanding to take over all the Russian churches and substitute a Ukrainian order of service. Though he himself spoke Ukrainian with his parishioners, the priest had trained in a Russian seminary and his services were in Church Slavonic. Faith was faith: he had been ordained to give the service in the ancient language and to give his obedience to the patriarchs of Moscow and Constantinople. The new patriarch in Kiev was an upstart. It was all politics, he said, and it would all end badly. His son was choirmaster in the cathedral at Vinnitsa, the biggest town nearby, and the Ukrainians were demanding that the church be handed over to them. Their son was prepared to fight at the church door, if need be. 'People will be killed,' the priest's wife said gloomily. After some silence together, companionable and thoughtful, they stood and bowed to the icons, blessed themselves and us and walked home through the dark to their house.

Next morning, I got my first daylight view of the village. I was at the well outside, winding up water to wash in and make tea. A small group of children passed by with satchels on their way to school. In the vegetable garden of the cottage opposite, an old woman in bedroom slippers cut off the head of a cabbage for soup and before turning back indoors stared silently at me. An old man drove past in a cart, flicking his whip against the withered flanks of his old horse. On the back of the cart sat two farmworkers in tattered blue suits and muddy boots. They stared at me too. An ancient woman, bent and crooked, struggled by leaning heavily on a stick. A damp fog clung close to the ground.

I walked down the track to the river, coiling between the fields, hazy with the fog. It was how Lena and I had located Kroupodernitsa on the map in Kiev, by tracing our fingers along the River Ross until we found the village by name. I have a photograph of my grandfather as a teenager, in a naval cap rowing his sisters in long print dresses, out beneath the railroad bridge, on a summer afternoon in the early 1890s. The railway bridge was nowhere to be seen. A few geese pecked about amid the discarded bottles and scraps of sodden paper on the water-bank. I stared out across the river and thought of my grandmother, how she hated this place.

Walking along the bank, I came across an old two-story brick building, with machinery whirring and grinding inside. Farmwomen in kerchiefs were shouldering grain out of sacks into a tin shute: the grain sluiced down into the mill and a white cone of flour spilled out at the other end. Other women were scooping it into sacks. Dust, cobwebs and flour coated the beams, windows and machines. Flour drifted down through the air onto my shoes. The shutes were of recent hammered tin, but the mill machinery itself was much older.

When I rubbed the flour off from the name-plates on the old iron stanchions, the words 'Dresden 1886' and 'Leipzig 1887' came up beneath my fingers. This was my great-grandfather's flour mill, once powered by the dams and mill-races on the river, and now by electricity from a Soviet-era power plant. The machines he had purchased in Germany and brought back by rail, at what must have been astronomical expense, were still milling the village's grain a century later.

All of the land around the village, once owned by my great-grandfather and farmed by my grandfather, was now farmed by the kolkhoz, the collective farm. The hedgerows and trees which in the photographs of the family album criss-crossed the fields a century ago had been cut down to consolidate the arable land and make way for large-scale machinery. Now, on the other side of the river bank, the black soil fields rolled away to the horizon, bare and empty. The manager of the collective farm, a young man in shirtsleeves, with smooth hands and the white unweathered face of a city person, was watching the milling of the grain. Through Lena, who by then had joined me, I asked him why, now that the Ukraine was independent and nominally committed to free enterprise, he didn't turn the land over to the local people. He shrugged amiably. Who do I give it to? Who is there? He gestured at the huge bare fields across the river. Who would have the capital to farm such large fields? The women shouldering the sacks of flour off the shutes listened and concurred. Most of their sons had moved to the city. It was a village of old women, they said, though most of them seemed robust enough to run a farm on their own, if they could be given a tractor, tools, seed and a line of credit to some bank.

I though of the peasants in the family album, of the estate steward Rudnitsky, with his weather-beaten face, full grey beard and three-quarter-length frock coat over high-topped boots, posing for Peggy Meadowcroft's Box Brownie with his

son and his family in front of a white-washed thatched
cottage. Or of the Sessoueff family, grouped beneath a tree
in front of their cottage, mother in black kerchief and full
skirts, children in white Ukrainian embroidered dresses,
wealthy enough to give their girls necklaces; wealthy enough
for Mr Sessoueff to wear well-shined boots. Peggy had
inscribed their names in white ink beneath their pictures in
the album. They could have taken over the land after my
great-grandmother died in the winter of 1917; through
Lena, I began asking what had happened to the Rudnitskys,
to the Sessoueffs. One old lady told us bleakly to go look in
the village graveyard. There, near the green fence was the
tomb of old Sessoueff, with the date of his death chiselled in:
1924. But what about Rudnitsky and his able-bodied son,
with a bronzed face and a full splay of whiskers?
'Repressed,' the school-teacher was to tell me. 'All
repressed.' And when, I wanted to know? Thirty-one,
thirty-two. The priest confirmed it too. He hadn't been
there then, but the old women who came to his church
remembered it only too well. Teams came down from
Kiev, looking for the people they called the grainhoarders,
the bloodsuckers, the vampires; they requisitioned all the
available local food for the towns and turned the poorest
labourers against the small holders, or kulaks as they were
known; then they arrested the kulaks and took them away.
The hedgerows were plowed under; the big fields were
laid out and the land was fully collectivized. The kulaks
who stood in the way – the Rudnitskys, the Sessoueffs,
especially, because they had once worked for the old
master – were driven away, imprisoned or shot.

Historians estimate that something like three million
Ukrainians died of hunger, when the land was collectivized, between 1931 and 1933. A further million were
killed during the purges of intellectuals and party officials.
An additional 2–3 million kulaks were deported to

Siberia. The peasant culture of small farmers and labourers which my grandfather grew up among was extermi-
nated. This was when fear came to the village. And it has
never left. Walking along the sandy tracks towards the big
house on the hill, past the low cottages, behind the rickety
picket fences, some in wattle and daub, some still
thatched, as they were in an English Nanny's photographs
at Easter 1915, I began to see the old women bent over
their cabbage patches in the back gardens, tossing onion
skins and cabbage tops onto their compost, as survivors of
a man-made catastrophe.

After breakfast, Lena and I headed off in search of the
family house. Great-grandfather built it in the 1860s as a
summer place for his family, when he was Czar Alexander
II's Ambassador in Constantinople. When his sons married, he added wings to house them and their children.
Vast family gatherings were held here at Easter and in the
summer months, when the brothers and sisters would
make the journey south from Moscow and Petersburg. In
the pictures, it was a capacious, plain two-story stuccoed
and whitewashed mansion, with a ceremonial front porch
and balconies on the first-floor bedrooms carved in the
ornate Ukrainian style. There were ornamental gardens
with fish-ponds, and gravel paths through woods and
benches where the old man and his wife could sit and rest
on their walks during his long and embittered retirement
from office after being dismissed by the Czar in 1882.

The gardens were nowhere to be seen; the high stone
wall which marked if off from the village had been torn
down or pillaged for bricks; one of the wings built for the
sons had burnt down, and the other was in ruins. But the
main house still stood: recognizably the same, though the
Ukrainian gingerbread balconies and roof decorations
were gone. I walked up the drive towards the covered
front porch. Was this really the courtyard where Mitro,

the bearded coachman, used to draw up the family *shara-ban* – the charabanc – the old man used to take when he went on afternoon tours of his farms? Seventy-five years ago, my father's brothers – Dima, Alec, Lionel – were photographed, just here, half-kneeling in the driveway, wearing their sailor-suits and squinting at Peggy's camera, their heads shaved close for the summer.

I had been lucky; many mansions were burned or sacked at the Revolution. This one had been converted into the village school, and the teachers were on the steps to greet me. A girl in a peasant costume and Ukrainian head-dress, made of purple and pink plastic flowers, curt-seyed and presented me with the traditional greeting pre-sents: a round loaf of bread, decorated with pastry leaves and a pastry sheaf of grain. Word of my arrival must have spread in the night: one of the teachers had baked it before coming to work. The little girl also carried a bowl of salt. I took a piece of the bread, dipped it in the salt and took a bite. This was how my grandmother was greeted when she arrived here as my grandfather's bride, in 1902. From cottage to cottage, the marriage procession went, and each family made them a ceremonial gift of bread and salt.

They led me into the house, a bare, rough-planked place built by peasant carpenters, now smelling of children and carbolic soap and fresh whitewash. My uncle Dima had described the interior to me many times: his grand-father's study with its crossed swords and its portrait of Gladstone; the heavy, cozy and overstuffed sitting-room where his grandmother received her grandchildren, no longer the fine young woman who charmed Disraeli at Hatfield House, but instead a stout *babushka* always clad in loose-flowing robes and a headscarf. She was the pre-siding matriarch of a large estate but in the photographs of that last family Easter in 1915, she seems more tender than imposing. In one picture, her five- and six-year-old grandchildren, my uncles Dima and Lionel, have clambered onto her lap, and she holds them by the waist. They entwine their fingers in hers. It seemed uncanny, and in some way very sad to be standing on the spot where that particular picture was taken, of an old lady bouncing her grandchildren on her knee, an old lady whose grandfather had led Russia's armies against Napoleon and whose grandchildren were to die in exile at the end of the 20th century five thousand miles away.

I was lost in thought when one of the teachers asked me whether it was true that Honoré de Balzac, the great French author, had stayed the night here. I said I doubted it. But then the director of the school told *me* something I did not know, though how the story had passed into the myths of the village I never learned. Apparently, my great-grandfather's daily companion and friend was the village priest. They walked in the gardens, lunched together, discussed the Scriptures. In his old age, glory gone, health declining, he became even more devout, kneeling down on the floor of the church, head bowed, considering his many sins. And in his loneliness and perhaps depression, he had only the company of his wife and the venerable old village priest. One day, in the year 1908, the servants came to him in great distress to announce that the old priest had died in his sleep. My great-grandfather heard the news in the downstairs hall and turned, so the schoolteacher told me, to make his way upstairs to his study, where he wished to be left alone. At the foot of the stairs, he fell and, while the servants made frantic attempts to revive him, he died. Here, right here, the schoolteacher said, as we mounted the plain-planked stairs.

In room after room, where my uncles must have slept as boys, children of six and seven were learning the Ukrainian language. One of these rooms, under the eaves, was Peggy Meadowcroft's: I have one of her snapshots of it, with heavy stuffed furniture, and wildflowers in three jars, and a white embroidered shawl draped over one chair, and the light streaming in through the windows and bleeding contrast out of the picture. Now it was filled with children bent over their school work, sneaking the occasional glance at me. Where they once learned about Yuri Gagarin and the heroic Soviet spacemen, they were now being taught about the Ukrainian bard Taras Shevchenko. In the next room, the children were learning patriotic songs, and for my benefit, one girl stood and sang an exceptionally bloody song (so Lena whispered to me) about the Ukrainian Cossacks overthrowing Moscow's yoke. She sang about the bloody revenge of the Cossack horsemen in a small, high-piping voice and smiled sweetly and curtseyed when she had finished.

Another upstairs room had been strewn with grasses, as peasant cottages of old were meant to be, and decorated as a museum of Ukrainian peasant culture. But the remains of that culture were beggarly: an old wooden spinning wheel, half-rotted away, a wooden rake, a blackened iron samovar.

In the school auditorium, decorated with pictures of Soviet pioneers, heroes of the Patriotic War, and once my great-grandparents' drawing room, I was asked to address the pupils. The children, the boys' blond hair clipped short, the girls with little red bows in their braids, looked at me in baffled silence. With Lena translating, I told the children that I was the great-grandson of the man who built this house. I wanted to bridge the enormous distance of time which separated them from my past, but I found myself unable to find the words. I was as strange to them as if I had stepped out of one of Peggy Meadowcroft's photographs. So I merely said that I was grateful to the teachers for keeping the house intact and I then presented the school with copies of images from the Russian Album. Afterwards, they crowded around and pointed and stared at the photographs of women in long dresses and children, their age, in sailor-suits and short trousers.

After the revolution, Aunt Mika, a gentle and retiring spinster who ran a dispensary in the village and then a hospital for wounded soldiers from the Galician front stayed on at the estate. Perhaps in the 1920s, perhaps later in the 1930s, when collectivization began, she was spirited away to Kiev where she went into a nunnery for her protection. From there a postcard reached my grandfather in the middle of the war in his sister's handwriting, telling him that in the village they still remembered the choirmaster.

The peasants might have remembered, but it was also true that they had looted the house from the attic to the cellar. Not a stick of the furniture in the album photographs, not a picture on the walls, not a plate, not a piece of embroidered linen, not a samovar or a spoon remained. One old man did rush back to his house and pulled out a battered reproduction of a photograph of the Count, taken when he was already a bent old man. How such a photograph had survived, in a peasant's house, throughout the Stalin time, I never learned.

By the 1930s, so the headmaster told me, the house had been divided up into a dwelling house for many of the village families. Then, someone said, it had become an orphanage. During the Second World War, the area had been occupied by the Germans, but the village itself had not been touched and the house itself did not seem to have been requisitioned or used as a German barracks.

The south-central Ukraine was once home to Jewish small farmers, peddlers and dealers. One of the teachers took me aside to a window, out of earshot of the children, and told me – in broken German – that he had witnessed something terrible in Pogribisce in 1941. The *Einsatz-gruppen* killing squads had followed the *Wehrmacht*'s advance through the Ukraine and systematically destroyed the Jewish civilization which had shared these valleys with Orthodox people for centuries. The teacher had been a boy then, but in a clearing outside Pogribisce, he had seen shootings, open pits, bodies piled upon each other and work teams shovelling sand and lime over them. Why he had seen this, what he was doing there, whether he had seen it at all or had heard it from someone who had, he did not say. The sand, he said, kept moving after the bodies were covered over.

The church bells began tolling in the village. Lena and I said goodbye to the teachers and the children and we walked down to the church, where the choir and parishioners were assembling for a service. The sexton and his son were up in the tower making the bells ring out over the valley. The building, standing amidst a grassy churchyard full of graves, was built of striped layers of sand and red-coloured brick, topped by three lead-coloured domes. In the churchyard, I found a small chapel and ducking my head low went in. Still wet from a recent mop was a small granite slab inscribed with the words 'Count Paul Ignatieff, 1909–1911'. This was the grave of the child who died of typhoid in Eupatoria, the one whose picture my grandmother kept by her bedside all her life: my uncle. And behind the church, surrounded by shade trees was a ten-foot wooden cross atop a granite plinth. By the heavy black anchors which ringed the plinth, I knew at once whose grave this must be: the sailor in the family, my grandfather's youngest brother, Vladimir, who died at the battle of Tsushima, in the Russo-Japanese War of 1905.

And now the sexton had come down from the tower and had opened the large plank doors to the church proper. Lights streamed through the windows onto the newly swept mosaic floor. On the pillars, on the vaulted ceiling high over my head the saints stared down, newly painted, in ochre and crimson, blue and gold. Old ladies walked from icon stand to icon stand lighting candles. The priest's wife lowered the huge candelabra down from the dome, lit all the candles one by one, and briskly hoisted it back into place. The choir – half a dozen men and women from nearby Vinnitsa, directed by the priest's son – took up its position in the choir stalls in the nave. A small collection of parishioners, mostly old bent ladies with sticks, took up their places, leaning against the pillars at the back, crossing themselves.

I stood alone under the dome, with Lena behind me, and the choir began to sing the *pannihida*, the memorial service for the dead. The priest had asked Lena for the names of all my family, and now in his prayers, he mentioned them one by one, my mother, my two children, my father, my uncles, my grandparents and great-grandparents, Russian names, English names mixed in with the benedictions and formulas of Church Slavonic, the names lifted by the choir's voices and carried aloft into the uppermost reaches of the church.

When the singing was done, the priest came over and asked me to turn around and say something to the choir and to the parishioners. I thanked them for remembering my family in prayer, for singing their names and for keeping their graves. Three old women edged closer. One took my hand and began to kiss it. Another tugged my sleeve and said through broken teeth, and in a hoarse whisper, that she was one of the village children, one of those who had been a godchild of Aunt Mika. She brought mushrooms to the kitchen door. She remembered the smell of jam cooking. She wanted me to know how bad it had been afterwards, and then she began to cry, helplessly, touching her old face with both hands, her mouth a black circle of lamentation, at once the kerchiefed young girl she had once been and also, and irremediably, the broken survivor of all the horror that had followed.

The priest led me away, out of the church, through the graveyard. The doors to the crypt had been opened, and the light streamed into the low, vaulted space, strewn with grasses, with fresh field flowers in pickle jars in front of the icons, and all the candles lit. There, directly in front of me, exactly as the photographs led me to expect, was the grave of my great-grandfather, a white marble slab on a black basalt base, engraved with his name, his military rank of General Adjutant, his court title of Count, the dates 1832–1908, and beneath that the names of the two treaties he had signed in the Czar's name: Peking 1860, and San Stefano 1878. In several places the lettering was bisected by vigorous slashes cut deep into the stone by some exceedingly sharp blade. I ran my finger tip along the cold incisions in the basalt over the Ignatieff name. They used your great-grandfather's tomb as a butcher's block, the priest said, From the 1930s until the early 1950s, when the priest arrived, animal carcasses – hogs and cattle mostly – were unloaded in the churchyard out-side and dragged into the crypt to be cut into sections. It wasn't hard to imagine the cleaver striking sparks on the gore-smeared stone and the blood of animals running on the pavings at my feet. The priest made a rueful click of his tongue, as if to commiserate. But I wasn't sure that it was a profanation exactly, or if it was, I didn't feel it as such. I felt better knowing what had happened. Instead of there being only silence and darkness and the slow gather-ing of dust since 1917, and nothing known for certain about any of the time intervening, there had been, at least for some years, a butcher with knives and cleavers cutting up the hogs and cattle of Kroupodernitsa on the old Count's grave. I had come in search, not of what the village had once been – since I knew that already from the Russian Album – but of what had happened after, after the time frozen in those snapshots, when the pose was broken, when the smiles faded on every face. Now I knew something certain about what had happened *after*. The grave had been a butcher's block. The cuts across its surface seemed to stand for everything that had happened here since the moments frozen in the album at Easter 1915. And despite everything, the cuts did not run all that deep. The letters of our name were still visible. The blood had washed away. The butcher and his meat had gone. The grave was still there.

On each side of his tomb, there were jagged breaks in the tile flooring, and where the titles should be, beaten earth strewn with wildflowers. As I edged back the flowers with my shoe, the earthen space where the tiles had been ripped up assumed the outline shape of a shrouded body. I realized I was staring down at graves, roughly and hastily dug through the earthenware tiles into the damp earth. But whose graves? The priest knew. One was my grandfather's sister, Aunt Katia. My grandfather had brought her home himself from the Eastern Front, where she had died nursing soldiers in a hospital train in 1915. For some reason, it being in the middle of the war, he had not been able to raise a burial stone over her body. And now she lay there, beneath the crypt, beside her father – and still uncovered. On the other side of his tomb lay a second, more or less identical body-shaped tear in the earthenware tiles. This must be where my great-grandmother had been laid, when she died in January 1917. Again, my grandfather must have meant to raise a stone over her head. I wanted to think it had been ordered, even paid for. But the revolution had intervened. The family went into exile. Who, but Aunt Mika, alone and penniless, was left to supervise the laying of the stones?

I had a thick bundle of roubles in my pocket. I handed them to the priest and asked him – through Lena – to find a mason in Pogribisce who would lay some stone on these naked graves. Father Sergei looked at me for a moment, considered the wad of red rouble notes in his hand, pondered the various possibilities, slipped the money into a pocket beneath his surplice and nodded. I went away believing nothing would happen.

I returned a year later, unannounced with a television crew, to make a documentary about Ukrainian independence in a series called *Blood and Belonging*. I was in the area, I said disingenuously, and wanted to drop in. The priest's wife leaned up on tiptoes and kissed me fiercely on both cheeks. The priest let me shake his hand, but continued to watch me with his small eyes. We drank vodka and everything, they said, was just the same, thank God, except that everyone was older and just as poor as ever. Eventually, I asked to go down to the crypt. The priest got the keys and led the way down the muddy track to the church. When the iron doors were swung back and the candles beneath the icons were lit, there beside the black basalt slab of my great-grandfather were two simple grey marble slabs on either side, covering the naked place where the women had lain for eighty years. I could not have wished it done better, and I said so. There and then, the priest and his wife, and the sexton and his wife, who had come along too, began singing the *pannihida*, and in the damp darkness, with the blue icon's lamp light glittering on the tombs of my family, they sang the words which end the Orthodox service for the dead – Eternal Memory, Eternal Memory Grant Him O Lord – and I felt, as tears finally came, that I had laid to rest at last not only my Russian ancestors but my father as well.

Michael Ignatieff
August 1997

INDEX

Adams Brown, Isobel, 155, 157
Aegean Sea, 52
Alberta, Canada, 159
Alexander I, 26, 27, 50–1
Alexander II, 42, 50
Alexander III, 24, 55–6, 59–60
Alexandra Pavlovna, Tsarina of Russia, 38, 86–7, 95, 100–1, 105
Amur, river, 8, 44
Andrassy, Count, 52
anti-semitism, 24, 58–9, 80, 82, 96
Atarbekov, 128, 131
Austria-Hungary, 52

Baedeker's guide to Russia, 19, 25
Bakunin, Mikhail, 45
Balkan atrocities, 49
Baltic Sea, 42
Barthes, Roland, 6
Beauchamps, 150–60
Belilovsky, Dr, 155–7
Bessarabia, 47, 51, 58
Bismarck, Count von, 49, 52, 61, 87
Black Sea, 17, 50, 120, 142
Bokhara, 43, 54
Bolsheviks, 117, 124, 126, 128–30, 133, 175
Bosnia, 47, 50, 51, 93
Bossibrod, 54, 72, 99
Boxer Rebellion, 74
Brest Litovsk, treaty of, 148
British Columbia, 161
Bucharest, 51
Bulgaria, 13, 47, 51, 52, 142, 156, 181

Canada, 5, 11, 158–85
Cannes, 33, 65, 66
Cap d'Antibes, 70–1
Caspian Sea, 17, 43, 120
Castellot, Monsieur, 53, 60, 61, 62, 68
Catherine II, 9, 28, 115
Charcot, J. M., 62, 114
China, 8, 44
Citizen, The (newspaper), 24
Conference of Berlin, 52
Constantinople, 46, 50, 51, 52, 143, 144–5, 180
Corps des Pages, 41–2
Cossacks, 10, 43, 79, 109, 112, 124–5, 133
Crimea, 29, 41, 50, 84–5, 123, 139
Crimean War, 42, 49, 51

Dardanelles, 48, 50, 51, 52
Darier, Monsieur, 17, 110, 111, 116
Decembrists, 41, 56
Demian, 87, 110, 111, 114, 116, 118
Demidoff, Prince, 91
Denikin, General, 123, 139, 144
Disraeli, Benjamin, 48, 52, 61, 99
doctors, 34, 36, 37
Dostoevsky, Fyodor, 42
Doughino, 19, 21, 26–8, 36–8, 72–3, 118
Doukhobours, 161
Dresden, 18, 69
Duma, 4, 96, 102, 104, 109, 112, 116

Ekaterinadar, 141

Elliot, Sir Henry, 47
Engalicheff family, 40
Essentuki, 125
Eupatoria, 84

Fourstatskaya street, 17, 109–13, 169
Freud, S., 61, 62

Galernaya street, 86
Galitzine family, 92
Gatchina, 64, 94
Gladstone, W. E., 60
Gorchakov, Prince, 49, 52
Goremikin, I. L., 95, 100
Grafton, HMS, 140
Grant family, 8
Grinevetsky, 55, 65, 83
Gueh, Xenia, 138

Hart House, 172–3
Hastings, 150
Hatfield House, 48
Herzegovina, 51
Herzen, Alexander, 42, 45
Hoover, Herbert, 157
Huanchaco, SS, 140–1, 144

Ignatieff, Alec, 81, 84, 92, 115, 137,
    154–6, 157, 163, 168–70
Ignatieff, Alexis (governor of Tver),
    77, 80, 94, 96
Ignatieff, Alison Grant, 10, 11, 163
Ignatieff, General A. A. ('Uncle
    Alyosha'), 17, 97, 145–6, 178
Ignatieff, Ekaterina (née Galitzine), 45,
    46–8, 55, 61, 65, 72, 78, 98–9,
    108–9
Ignatieff, Florence Hargreaves, 14,
    174–80, 183
Ignatieff, George, 4, 10–11, 13, 19, 87,
    90, 103, 119, 136, 146–8, 152, 156,
    157, 159, 160, 161, 163, 170, 172,
    181–3
Ignatieff, Helen Fraser, 163, 182–3

Ignatieff, Katia, 65, 73–4, 78, 94, 97
Ignatieff, Kolya, 94, 97, 151, 154, 156,
    182
Ignatieff, Lionel, 87, 119, 149, 156,
    157, 163, 164, 166–8, 170, 177, 183
Ignatieff, Marjorie Adams, 163,
    168–70
Ignatieff, Mika, 73, 94, 99, 108, 124,
    169, 179–80
Ignatieff, Mika (Farer), 12, 179
Ignatieff, Natasha Mestchersky
    (1877–1944), birth, 22; childhood,
    21–33; courtship and marriage,
    67–70; childbirth, 74–5; marriage,
    87–8; attitude to revolution, 112–5;
    and release of her husband, 127–30;
    and Peggy Meadowcroft, 90, 142,
    147; as mother, 157; on exile,
    157–8; in Quebec, 164–5; her
    memoirs, 13–14, 20, 164; death,
    183
Ignatieff, Nicholas (1832–1908), birth,
    42; early career, 42–3; expedition to
    Khiva and Bokhara, 43; expedition
    to Peking, 43–5; marriage, 45;
    ambassador to Constantinople,
    47–50; in Russo-Turkish War,
    50–2; as Minister of the Interior,
    55–60; retirement, 64–5; death, 83
Ignatieff, Nicholas (1904–52), 12, 13,
    40, 43, 60, 65, 74, 79, 110, 121–2,
    126, 133, 147, 154, 158–9, 161–2,
    163, 170–3, 183
Ignatieff, Nicholas ('little Nick'), 183
Ignatieff, Paul N. (1797–1879), 40–6,
    50–1
Ignatieff, Paul (1870–1945), birth, 46;
    childhood, 50–61; adolescence,
    61–3; illness, 61, 114, 122, 149;
    education, 62–3; farming career, 63;
    military service, 64; courtship and
    marriage, 67–70; chairman of Kiev
    zemstvo, 75–80; governor of Kiev,
    80–3; relations with father, 82; as

INDEX

deputy Minister of Agriculture, 84, 87–8; as Maltsev heir, 91–2; as Minister of Education, 94–105; resignation and dismissal, 104–5; as president, Russian Red Cross, 113, 146, 156–7, 162; arrest, imprisonment and release, 125–33; as Sussex farmer, 150–3; in retirement, Quebec, 162; death, 183

Ignatieff, Paul (1907–09), 81, 85

Ignatieff, Vladimir, 68, 77

Ignatieff, Vladimir ('Dima'), 78, 85, 92, 121, 127, 133, 137, 152, 157–9, 162, 163, 164, 173–81, 183

Irkutsk, 44

Jews, 8, 58, 78, 81, 95, 96

Karamzin, Nicholas, 9, 10, 26, 118

Kerensky, 123

Khiva, 43, 54

Khrushchev, Nikita, 11, 16

Kiev, 54, 55, 75–83

Kishinev, 83

Kislovodsk, 17, 118, 120–6, 133

Korea, 77

Koulakoff, 110, 116, 118, 125, 135, 140

Krivoshein, 84, 87, 94, 100, 101

Kroupodernitsa, 19, 50, 52, 54–5, 61, 62, 65, 72–3, 82, 97–9, 108–9, 124, 169

Kutuzov, Mikhail, 45, 61

La Flandre, 145, 180

Lenin, V. I., 17, 56, 117, 125, 146, 178

Leningrad, 12, 17

Lipovetz, 72–3

London, 42, 147–9, 163

Lower Canada College, 160, 161

Lytton, Lord, 47

Macedonia, 52

Malevsky, Colonel, 151, 154, 156

Maltsev family, 40

Manchuria, 74, 77

Marseilles, 145

Matisse, Henri, 17

McGill University, 163

Meadowcroft, Peggy, 89, 98, 103, 110, 120, 122, 124, 133, 134, 135, 136, 138, 139, 140–1, 147–56

Mestchersky, Princess Maria, 21, 34–8, 35, 67

Mestchersky, Prince Nicholas, 22, 23, 33–4

Mestchersky, Peter, 25, 33, 35, 67, 134

Mestchersky, Sasha, 25, 29, 35, 38, 153

Mestchersky, Vera, 21

Mestchersky, Prince Vladimir, 24

Miliukov, P., 105

Mineralni Vodi, 140, 179

Misdroy, 88

Misetsky, Judge, 151, 156

Mogilev, 105

Montenegro, 47, 50

Montreal, 160–72

Montrose, SS, 160

Moscow, 18, 23, 30, 38, 66, 100, 176

Muraviev, Count, 45

Nabokov, Vladimir (novelist), 7–8

Nabokov, Vladimir (father of novelist), 63, 83, 94

Napoleonic Wars, 41, 45

Nechaev, Professor, 127

Nechaev-Maltsev, Y., 91

Nice, 18, 33, 52, 66

Nicholas I, 41

Nicholas II, 8, 38, 64, 84, 91, 94, 100–5

Nizhni Novgorod, 55

Novodévichy cemetery, 17

Novorossisk, 139–42

Odessa, 54, 82, 139, 140

Okhrana, 56, 80, 82

Orenberg, 43
Orthodox church, 11, 47, 58–9, 71, 78–9, 81, 98, 148, 167
Ottawa, 168
Ottoman empire, 46–9, 51
Ouman, 72, 73
Ourousoff family, 37
Oxus, river, 43

Panin, Nikita, 22, 27
Panin, Peter, 22
Paris, 14, 55, 56, 62, 65, 145–6, 157
Parkin family, 8
Pearson, L. B., 11
peasants, 36–8, 56–7, 62–3, 71, 73, 75, 80, 87, 93
Peking, 10, 44, 54, 83
People's Will, 56
Petrograd (St Petersburg), 9, 40, 57, 84–5, 86 *passim*
photography, 2–6, 86, 184–5
Piatigorsk, 128–30, 133
Plevna, 50, 51, 56
Pobedonostsev, K., 59–60
pogroms, 58, 78, 83
Poland, 97, 131
Porechie, 53
Preobrajensky Guards, 41, 64, 83, 94, 111, 151, 154
Protopopoff, 104
provisional government, 113, 115
Pugachev, E., 9, 22
Pushkin Museum, 17
Putney, 146–56

Rachinsky, Professor, 37
Rasputin, Grigori, 96, 100, 107
Red Cross, Russian, 113, 146, 156–7
revolution of 1905, 78–80
revolution of March 1917, 111–18
revolution of October 1917, 123
Richmond, Quebec, 173–5, 183
Ross, river, 54
Russo-Japanese War, 74, 76–7, 93

Russo-Turkish War, 8, 13, 36, 50–2

St Paul's School, 150–5
Salisbury, Lord, 47
San Stefano, treaty of, 51, 52, 56, 83
Saturday Night, magazine, 171
self, the, 1–9
Serbia, 48–50, 51
Shanghai, 44
Sheremetieff, Countess, 23, 36
Shipka Pass, 51, 52
Shkuro, Andrei, 124, 133, 134
Siberia, 41, 44, 45, 123
Slavonic Society, 60, 67
Slavophiles, 49, 52, 59, 63, 95
Smolensk, 8, 25
Socialist Revolutionaries, 80, 129–31, 133
Sontag, Susan, 3
Soviet Union, 11, 12, 16–18, 123, 158, 171–3
Stalin, J. V., 16, 17, 56, 171, 178
Stolypin government, 84
Sultan Abdul Aziz, 48
Sussex, 14, 150–9

Tauride Palace, 96, 109
Tiesenhausen, Countess, 41
Titanic, ss, 88
Tolstoy, 37, 63, 68
Tonia, 89, 125, 135
Toronto, 8, 162, 166, 173
Trotsky, L., 123
Tsarskoe Selo, 92, 94, 97, 100, 103, 104, 109, 117
Tsushima, 78, 83
Tsvetaev, Ivan, 91
Turkey, 47–52
Tursky, I., 126, 128
typhoid, 84–5

University of Toronto, 162, 172

INDEX

Upper Melbourne, Quebec, 13,
162–5, 173–5, 183
Ussuri, river, 44

Vaclav, 125, 136, 140
Varna, 142
Victoria, Queen, 48
Vienna, 53
Vladivostok, 45, 74, 77, 78
Volga, river, 55
Vybiti, 92, 103

Wassiltchikoff, Boria, 92, 117, 151,
154
Wassiltchikoff, Sonia, 25, 30, 86, 92,
103, 116, 151, 156
Women's Battalion, 122–3
Wrangel, General, 123, 138–9

zemski sobor, 59
zemstvos, 56, 75–6, 79–80, 96, 102,
108
Zouroff family, 40